GW01316228

Alphabet of classical dance

Alphabet of classical dance

Nadezhda Bazarova and Varvara Mey

Translated from the Russian by Simon André

Edited by Richard Glasstone

Dance Books
Cecil Court   London

First published in Leningrad in 1983
This translation published in 1987 by Dance Books Ltd., 9 Cecil Court,
London WC2N 4EZ

Translation © 1987 Dance Books Ltd

British Library Cataloguing in Publication Data

Bazarova, Nadezhda
   Alphabet of classical dance.
   1. Ballet
   I. Title   II. Mey, Varvara
   III Glasstone, Richard
   792.8′2   GV1788

   ISBN 0-903102-95-1

Design and production in association with Book Production
Consultants, 47 Norfolk Street, Cambridge.

Printed and bound by The Bath Press, Bath, England.

From the authors

The necessary prerequisites for the classical dance are: turned out legs, a high extension, suppleness, stability, a light, high jump, precise movement co-ordination and, last but not least, endurance and strength.

These are developed by daily exercise, through careful adherence to accepted rules and to established theatrical practice. The construction of the class is the same for the first class as for the following classes, the only difference being that in the first class the movements are executed separately and in the simplest of combinations. An exception to this rule is found at the very beginning of the study, when the basic elements of the movements are being assimilated. The lesson consists of exercises at the barre and exercises in the centre of the room. The latter are divided into exercises, adagio (combinations of poses of the classical dance), allegro and exercises on point.

The order of the exercises at the barre is the following: pliés, battements tendus, battements tendus jetés, ronds de jambe par terre, battements fondus or soutenus, battements frappés, battements doubles frappés, ronds de jambe en l'air, petits battements, battements développés, grands battements jetés. The exercises in the centre are executed in the same order as at the barre. After the exercises in the centre the adagio is introduced. After the adagio follows allegro: small and big jumps and, not less than two to three times a week, exercises on point. The lesson is begun with a march in a calm tempo, which is gradually accelerated, then returns to normal tempo, after which one starts with the exercises. The march brings the organism into working condition, setting the blood circulation and the respiratory system going.

In the first year the march is also useful in the centre, as a means of relaxation between static positions. The lesson is concluded with port de bras and with bends of the torso forwards, backwards and sideways. The port de bras restores the breathing and brings the organism back to a condition of calm.

The class lasts for two hours. In the first year, a large part of the time is used for the exercises at the barre; in the following year the exercises at the barre last no longer than forty-five

3

minutes. With every year the time for the exercises at the barre is reduced as a result of the acceleration of the tempo. The exercises in the centre are so constructed that there are at least twenty minutes left for allegro. When exercises on point are introduced, the number of allegro exercises is reduced. In order for the lesson to be productive the teacher should prepare the exercises in advance.

The given order of movements is compulsory mainly in the first year. Later on, the order of the movements depends on the age of the pupils and on their professional aptitude. Theatrical practice plays a considerable role in the artistic education of the future dancers. It is introduced in the second half of the first year. In accordance with the syllabus material, dance numbers are prepared. The correct choice of dance numbers, taking into consideration the abilities of the pupils and giving them simple assignments, develops a feeling for dancing and expressiveness. Theatrical practice in the following years is also based upon the annual syllabus.

In conclusion, we feel it our duty to express our deepest gratitude to Vera Mikhailovna Krasovskaya, who spent much time and work on the editing of our textbook and showed herself to be of invaluable help to us.

The First Year of Study

The exercises of the first class

The basic aim of the first class is the placement of the torso, legs, arms and head by means of the simplest classical training exercises, and the development of elementary movement co-ordination skills. When starting to show the exercises, it is necessary to explain the concept of the working leg and of the supporting leg. The supporting leg supports the whole body during movements, by taking its weight onto it.

The working leg is no longer weight-bearing, and is therefore free to execute the movement. The functions of the working leg are considerably more diverse than the functions of the supporting leg; nevertheless the concept 'supporting leg' and 'working leg' are to some degree relative, as it is the 'pulling up' of the supporting leg during the exercises which guarantees stability.

All exercises are executed with the right and with the left leg. In order to master the turnout of the legs, a series of exercises is first taught to the side, and afterwards to the front and to the back. At first, the exercises are taught facing the barre, holding it with both hands. Later on, the same exercises are executed standing beside the barre and holding it with one hand; the other arm is opened to the side in second position. The exercises are executed with the toe on the floor and in the air, at an angle of approximately 25°, 45° or 90°. This angle is formed by the supporting leg and the working leg, which is held in the air. Various classical exercises are preceded by various preparations, several movements demanding a particular preparatory position.

Dance is organically linked with music. Without music the execution of classical exercises is senseless. The tempo and the rhythmic design of the musical accompaniment at the beginning and at the end of the first year are not the same. While the movement is passing through the stages of preparatory exercises, the rhythmic design is simple; by the end of the year it has become more varied. From the very first lessons onwards, the students' sense of musical hearing should be nurtured. At the beginning, the student should be introduced to the time signatures – 2/4, 3/4 and 4/4 – simply by listening to the music, then by marching to it, ensuring that the steps coincide with the musical beat. When the pupils have mastered a simple march in 2/4 time, it is necessary to introduce them to different time signatures, varying the musical accompaniment, speeding up and slowing down the tempo, changing the musical beat, watching strictly the structure of the musical phrase.

The march in class should have a dancing quality; the step is light, going from the toe through the entire foot, with the feet slightly turned out. The body is 'pulled up', the shoulders are opened and lowered. The girls hold their skirts with their fingertips, preserving a rounded line in the arms, the boys hold their hands on their waist.

At the same time, also in the centre of the room, a start is made on the teaching of the arm positions, of course with musical accompaniment. Parallel with this, at the barre, the placement of the body is started.

The placement of the body
A correctly placed body is a guarantee of stability. The correct placement of the body (fig. 1) not only ensures stability, it also facilitates the development of the turnout of the legs and the suppleness and expressiveness of the body necessary in classical dance.

When beginning to work on the correct placement of the body, it is necessary to stand facing the barre, placing the hands on the barre, the elbows slightly bent and lowered. The hands rest freely upon the barre (without clutching it), opposite the centre of the body. The legs are in first position. The knees are strongly stretched. The shoulders are opened freely and lowered. The muscles around the pelvis are 'pulled up' in such a manner that the body is straight, light and slender. This position is sustained until the end of the musical phrase.

fig. 1
The placement of the body

Remarks The 'pulling up' of the body determines the freedom of the hip joints, thus facilitating the development of turnout. The habit of keeping the body 'pulled up' becomes a skill which is one of the conditions of creative discipline in dance.

The placement of the body is initially to be taught in first position, afterwards in second, third and fifth positions.

The time signature is 4/4 or 3/4. The character of the music is even, legato. The position is held for a period of eight or sixteen bars.

The positions of the legs

In the classical dance there are five positions of the legs. At first the positions are taught in the centre, without full turnout. The turnout of the legs is introduced when placing the body. A description of the positions in their final form follows below (fig. 2). The positions of the legs are taught in the following order: first, second, third, fifth and fourth. The fourth position, being the most difficult one, is tackled last.

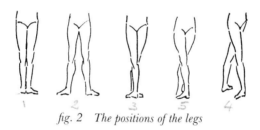

fig. 2   The positions of the legs

First position The feet, touching at the heels, are turned out with the toes pointing outwards, forming a straight line on the floor.

Second position Preserving the straight line as in first position, the heels are separated by about the length of one foot.

Third position In the same turned out position, the feet are crossed halfway, touching firmly.

Fifth position The feet, touching firmly, are crossed fully; the heel of one foot opposite the toe of the other.

Fourth position Preserving the turnout of the fifth position, the

7

feet do not touch; they are parallel to one another and are separated by the length of one foot.

The third, fifth and fourth positions are taught alternately with the right leg and with the left leg in front. The third position, being easier, serves as a preparation for the fifth. After mastering fifth position, the use of the third position is no longer necessary in classical dance lessons. The fourth position, when executed in the centre (and contrary to the other positions) demands a specific position of the arms and head. At first, fourth position is taught en face, later with épaulement; it is taken from fifth position.

Below follows an example for executing fourth position, once the arm positions, battement tendu and épaulement croisé and effacé have been mastered.

Example Initial position: fifth position, épaulement croisé, right leg in front, the arms in preparatory position, the head is turned to the right.

Two introductory chords. On 1&, the right leg, according to the rules for battement tendu, is stretched forward in croisée, the arms are raised in first position, the head inclines slightly to the left, the eyes are directed towards the hands. On 2&, the right heel is lowered to the floor, the toe is drawn back in order to reach the turned out position on the floor with the weight of the body evenly distributed over two legs. The right arm is opened in second position, the left arm remains in first and the head is turned to the right. The fourth position is held during the length of the musical phrase.

Two concluding chords. On 1&, the 'pull up' of the body is increased, and the weight of the body is transferred so that it is centred over the left leg; the right leg is stretched in front with the toe on the floor. On 2&, the right leg, according to the rules for battement tendu, returns into fifth position; both arms, the left one from first and the right arm from second position, are lowered into the preparatory position and the head remains turned to the right.

When beginning the study of fourth position in effacée, it is taken immediately from fifth position effacée.

Remarks When studying the positions of the legs, the following are essential: a 'pulled up' torso, freely opened and lowered shoulders, an exceptional stretch of the legs and an even position of the feet on the floor; it is not allowed to have excessive weight on the first toe. When studying second and fourth positions, it is important to centralise the body weight so that it is evenly distributed over both legs, and also to watch the level of shoulders and hips; a correct mastering of these positions is a guarantee for turnout.

At first the positions are studied separately; later, when battements tendus in all directions have been mastered, the transition from one position to another is executed by means of battement tendu.

Sustaining a given position for the entire duration of a musical phrase enables correct habits to be established, and develops a sense of discipline in the pupil.

The positions of the arms

The positions of the arms are studied in the centre from the first lessons onwards.

At first the position of the hands should be mastered. The edge of the thumb touches the second phalange of the middle finger, the other fingers are curved and freely arranged. This is only demanded during the initial stages, for as long as the movements of the students still lead to involuntary tension in the fingers. Later on, the hand acquires a relative freedom: the curve of the fingers is preserved, but the thumb no longer touches the middle finger: it is only directed towards it.

In the Leningrad School of Classical Dance there are three arm positions (fig. 3). They are studied with the legs in a natural position: the heels together, the toes pointing slightly to the side.

fig. 3   The positions of the arms

9

The torso is 'pulled up', the shoulders are lowered and opened. The position of the head is en face.

Preparatory position The arms are down, held freely with curved elbows and wrists in front of the body, forming an oval. The fingers are arranged as described above. The hands almost touch.

First position The arms, preserving their curve, are raised to the level of the diaphragm. During the movement they should be supported at two points: the elbows and the fingers, on one level. Before the study of second position, which is the more difficult, third position should be mastered. Its form is analogous to first position.

Third position The arms are raised from preparatory position to first position; preserving their curve, they are raised upwards, as if framing the head with an oval. The tendency of pupils to draw the arms backwards should be guarded against.

> *Exercise* The arms are raised from preparatory position to first position; from there, continuing the movement, they are raised to third position; from third position, they return to first and from first they are lowered into the preparatory position.

The exercise is also executed with one arm, which moves exactly opposite the centre of the body, the other arm remaining in preparatory position. The movements of the arms, here, as well as in the following exercises, should be smooth. The arms preserve their initial curve and move independently of the body.

The character of the musical accompaniment is smooth. The time signature is 4/4 or 3/4. The exercise is executed evenly, in four bars.

Only after first and third positions have been mastered will it be possible to start the study of second position.

Second position The arms are raised from the preparatory position into first. Preserving their curve, they are gradually opened to the side, starting the movement at the fingers. During this, the arms should be supported at two points, the elbows and the fingers, on one level. At the end of the movement, the arms are located a little in front of the body, continuing the line of the shoulders which are lowered and opened.

10

The tendency of the pupils to draw the arms backwards should be guarded against.

> *Exercise* The arms, which are opened in second position, are joined again in first position and lowered into preparatory position. The exercise is executed smoothly without accents. The time signature is 4/4 or 3/4.

During the first bar the arms are raised to first position. During the second bar they are opened to second position. During the third bar they are returned to first position. During the fourth bar they are lowered into the preparatory position.

After mastering second position, the arms are lowered immediately to the preparatory position.

> *Exercise* The arms, which are opened in second position, are turned with the palms facing downwards and, softening the elbows slightly, are lowered into the preparatory position, the fingers trailing slightly behind.
>
> The time signature is 4/4 or 3/4. During the first bar the arms are raised to first position. During the second bar they are opened to second position. During the third bar they remain in second position. During the fourth bar they are lowered to preparatory position.

The following exercise is more complicated.

> *Exercise* The arms, having been raised in third position, are opened to second position, preserving their curve and starting the movement at the fingers. They are then lowered immediately into the preparatory position. The time signature is 4/4, 3/4 or 6/8.

Remarks While executing the given exercises the arms should be free, without tension in the elbows and wrists. The shoulders do not take part in the movement, they are kept opened and lowered.

After mastering the three arm positions, the arm position which is used during exercises at the barre, holding it with one hand, is studied.

Standing at the barre, the hand is placed on top of it, a little in front of the body. The elbow is loosely bent and lowered. The free arm assumes the preparatory position. The legs stand in the desired position. The head is turned away from the barre. All the exercises at the barre are executed in this way, only now the movements of the head are also included. When the right hand is raised to first position, the head is inclined slightly towards the left shoulder, the eyes are directed towards the hand. When the arm opens to second position, the head, being raised, turns to the right, the eye direction follows the hand. When the arm is lowered into the preparatory position, the head remains turned to the right. If the arm is raised through first position into third, the head, turning to the right, is slightly raised, the eye direction following the hand. If the arm is opened to second position, the head is turned to the right. The movement of the head is free, the neck is not tense (fig. 4).

fig. 4   Préparation with the arm

It is necessary to watch attentively the level of the opened and lowered shoulders. The arm, which is executing the exercise, moves exactly opposite the centre of the torso; the hand which is resting on the barre does not change its initial position.

The time signature is the same as in the preceding exercises. Later on, the same exercises are given an artistic colouring. On the upbeat, the arms start the movement at the fingertips; bending the elbow slightly, they are opened sideways from the preparatory position.

The head, while turned to the side, inclines slightly, the eyes following the hand.[1] Returning again to the preparatory position, the arms execute the given movement.

This movement on the upbeat is at first included in the

[1] Later on this device will be described as 'the arms are opened'.

exercises at the barre; after it has been mastered, it is also executed in the centre.

Exercices à la barre

Battement tendu from first position

The denomination 'battements' is applied to many exercises of the classical dance. Literally, it means 'beating' or 'beat'; but here it refers to movements of the working leg. As a rule, the word battement is followed by another word, defining the character of the movement. Battements tendus – 'stretched movements' – produce a stretch of the entire leg, of the knee, instep and toes, developing the strength of the leg. At first, battement tendu is studied facing the barre and executed to the side, as in this direction it is easiest to cultivate and comprehend turnout.

Battement tendu to the side Initial position: first position. The torso is 'pulled up'. The knees are forcefully stretched. The hands are resting easily upon the barre, the elbows are lowered.

On 1 & 2, the stretched working leg slides with the entire foot along the floor to the side, the heel leaves the floor and, continuing to slide, the instep and toes are extended, reaching their maximum stretch. The toe touches the floor, the turned out heel is fully raised, thus stretching the instep. On 3 & 4, the position is held. On 1 & 2 of the second bar, the working leg, gradually transferring from the toe to the entire foot, returns with a sliding movement to first position. On 3 & 4, the position is held in order to consolidate a correct first position (fig. 5).

fig. 5   *Battement tendu to the side*   fig. 6   *Battement tendu to the front*   fig. 7   *Battement tendu to the back*

Battement tendu to the front Initial position: as described above.

On 1 & 2, the stretched working leg, maintaining the turnout of the heel, slides with the entire foot along the floor to the front; the heel leaves the floor and, continuing to slide, the instep and toes are extended, reaching their maximum stretch. The toe touches the floor, the heel is fully raised. In order to avoid a 'sickling' of the foot, only the first and second toes must touch the floor; the heel remains turned out. On 3 & 4, the position is held. On 1 & 2 of the second bar, the working leg, directing the toe to the back, and gradually transferring from the toe to the entire foot, returns to first position with a sliding movement. On 3 & 4, the position is held (fig. 6).

Battement tendu to the back Initial position: as described above.

On 1 & 2, the stretched working leg, directing the toe backward, slides with the entire foot along the floor, the heel leaves the floor and, continuing to slide, it is stretched to the back. Here it is particularly necessary to ensure that the shoulders and hips are level. Upon reaching the ultimate point, the working leg must be fully stretched and turned out, with forcefully stretched instep and toes. On 3 & 4, the position is held. On 1 & 2 of the second bar, the working leg, increasing the turnout of the heel, gradually transfers from the toe to the entire foot and returns with a sliding movement to first position. On 3 & 4 the position is held (fig. 7).

Remarks In battement tendu the working leg is moved exactly in a straight line, fixing the position of the heel opposite the initial position in each direction. The working leg is fully turned out in the hip-, knee- and ankle-joints. When moving the leg out of and into the position, it is important to keep the knee stretched. The supporting leg is taut and turned out. The torso is 'pulled up' and calm. The shoulders and hips remain level, especially when executing battement tendu to the front and to the back.

Having mastered battement tendu facing the barre, it is executed holding the barre with one hand.

Initial position: first position, the left arm is resting upon the barre, the right one is in preparatory position, the head is turned to the right. Two introductory chords. On 1, the right arm is raised in first position, the head inclines slightly towards the left shoulder, the eyes are directed towards the right hand. On 2, the right arm is opened in second position, the head turns to the right. With the beginning of battement tendu, the head turns en face. On two concluding chords, the right arm is closed in preparatory position and the head turns to the right.

At first, battements tendus are studied separately; having mastered them, they are executed consecutively, at the most eight times in each direction.

The time signature is 4/4. The character of the musical accompaniment is precise and lively. At first the movement is executed in two bars, afterwards in one. By the end of the year on each 1/4, beginning battement tendu on the upbeat. After mastering the exercise, the time signature is altered to 2/4; the movement is executed in one bar.

Demi plié

'Plier' means to bend or fold. Demi plié develops the turnout and the resilience of the legs. The initial position is first position.

On 1 & 2 &, the legs, increasing the turnout of the upper part, and directing the knees towards the toes, which are pointing outwards, bend slowly until the maximum bend of the ankle-joint is reached. The heels are placed firmly upon the floor, the body is straight and 'pulled up'. On 3 & 4, the legs, sustaining the turnout and the tension of the muscles, are stretched slowly until the initial position is reached. The 'pull up' of the torso is increased (fig. 8). Having mastered demi plié in first position, one proceeds to study it in all positions, in the following order: first, second, third, fifth. The fourth position, being the most difficult, is studied last.

fig. 8   Demi plié

Remarks In all positions the position of the foot on the floor is even; it is not allowed to put the weight on the first toe. In demi plié the heels must be pressed firmly into the floor, as this enables the development of the ankle joint. The body has to be straight and 'pulled up', with the shoulders and hips level. The body weight must be evenly centred over both legs. It is especially important to observe this in second and fourth positions.

At first, demi plié is studied facing the barre; later, holding on to the barre with one hand. The arms, one resting with the hand on the barre, one opened in second position, and the head, which is turned to the side, maintain their initial position during the execution of demi plié.

At first demi plié is executed separately, four times in each position; when it has been mastered, demi plié is executed consecutively in all positions, not more than twice in each one. The time signature is 4/4. The character of the musical accompaniment is flowing, *cantabile*. Demi plié is executed in one bar.

Demi rond de jambe par terre

Rond de jambe par terre is a circular movement of the leg on the floor. After having mastered the stretching of the leg, the exercises which develop the turnout and the mobility of the hip joint are studied. The first of these exercises is demi rond de jambe.

The initial position is first position, facing the barre. On 1 &, the working leg is stretched forward according to the rules for battement tendu. On 2 &, the toe, gliding along the floor describes an arc to second position until the heel of the working leg arrives opposite the heel of the supporting leg. On 3 &, the working leg, according to the rules for battement tendu, is closed in first position. On 4 &, first position is held.

On 1 & of the second bar, the working leg is stretched out in second position with the toe on the floor, according to the rules for battement tendu. On 2 &, the toe, sliding to the back along the floor, describes an arc until the heel of the working leg arrives opposite the heel of the supporting leg. The shoulders and hips remain level. On 3 &, the exercise is concluded in first position, according to the rules for battement tendu. On 4 &, first position is held.

The same exercise is also studied in the opposite direction. The initial position is first position. On 1&, the working leg is stretched to the back. On 2 &, the toe, gliding along the floor, describes an arc to second position so that the heel of the working leg arrives opposite the heel of the supporting leg. At the same time, the turnout of the entire leg is increased. On 3 &, the exercise is concluded in first position. On 4 &, first position is held. On 1 & of the second bar, the working leg is stretched in second position with the toe on the floor. On 2 &, the toe, gliding forward along the floor, describes an arc so that the heel of the working leg arrives opposite the heel of the supporting leg. On 3&, the exercise is concluded in first position. On 4 &, first position is held. Demi rond de jambe is executed 8 times in each direction.

Remarks It is necessary to watch the turnout and tension of both legs while executing demi rond de jambe. It is especially import-ant to watch the turnout and the tension of the working leg when moving it to the back. During the execution of rond de jambe, the torso is 'pulled up' and calm, the shoulders and hips are level.

The time signature is 4/4. The character of the musical accompaniment is smooth, legato. The exercise is executed in 2 bars.

Passé par terre

Passé par terre is, in this case, a sliding movement of the working leg along the floor. Passé par terre is an auxiliary movement in a number of exercises, and also an element of rond de jambe par terre when this is executed without stops. At first passé par terre is studied as an independent movement.

The initial position is first position, facing the barre. On two introductory chords, the working leg, according to the rules for battement tendu, is stretched to the back so that the heel arrives opposite the heel of the supporting leg.

On 1 &, 2 &, the working leg, increasing the turnout of the heel, is drawn with a gliding movement of the entire foot along the floor through first position and is stretched to the front with the toe on the floor, heel opposite heel. On 1 &, 2 &, of the following bar, the working leg, starting the gliding movement by drawing back the toe, is drawn with the entire foot along the floor through first position and is stretched to the back with the toe on the floor, heel opposite heel. The exercise is repeated until the end of the musical phrase.

Remarks In passé par terre, the working leg is particularly turned out and pulled up. During the passé through first position, the foot of the working leg is placed evenly on the floor, to avoid putting weight on the first toe. The supporting leg is pulled up and turned out. The torso is 'pulled up' and calm, the shoulders and hips are level.

The time signature is 2/4. The character of the musical accompaniment is smooth, legato. Each movement is executed evenly, on one bar.

Battement tendu from fifth position
After mastering battement tendu from first position one proceeds to study it from fifth position, first executing it facing the barre, after that, holding the barre with one hand. Here also, the aim is to develop the strength, tension and turnout of the legs.

Battement tendu to the side The initial position is fifth position, right leg in front. The torso is 'pulled up', the left hand rests upon the barre, the right arm is in the preparatory position. The head is turned to the right. On two introductory chords the arm is opened in second position.

On 1 &, while turning the head en face, the tense working leg, maintaining the turnout it had in fifth position, slides with the entire foot along the floor in the direction of second position. The heel is gradually leaving the floor. Continuing to slide, the instep and toes are fully stretched. The toe touches the floor, the turned out heel is fully raised. On 2 &, the position is held. On 1 & of the second bar, the working leg, gradually transferring from the toe to the entire foot, returns with a sliding movement to fifth position in front, accentuating the turnout of the position. On 2 &, the position is held. After that the movement is repeated, concluding it in fifth position behind. The exercise is continued alternating the fifth position in front and at the back.

Battement tendu to the front The initial position is as described above.

On 1 &, the tense working leg, maintaining the turnout of the heel, slides forward with the entire foot along the floor; as the heel leaves the floor it continues to slide, stretching the instep and the toes, reaching the ultimate stretch of the entire leg: the toe touches the floor, the heel is raised to the maximum. In order to prevent the foot from 'sickling' inwards, the first and second toes only touch the floor, the heel remains turned out. On 2 &,

the position is held. On 1 & of the second bar, the working leg, drawing the toe backwards, gradually transferring from the toe to the entire foot, returns with a sliding movement into fifth position, accentuating the turnout of the position. On 2 &, the position is held, etc.

Battement tendu to the back The intitial position is fifth position, the right leg behind, the left hand on the barre. On 1 &, the tense working leg, pointing the toe to the back, slides with the entire foot along the floor; as the heel leaves the floor it continues to slide and stretches to the back. Here one should particularly watch the level of the shoulders and hips. On reaching the ultimate point, the leg should be fully tense and turned out, with forcefully stretched instep and toes. On 1 & 2, the position is held. On 1 & of the second bar, the working leg, increasing the turnout of the heel and gradually transferring from the toe to the entire foot, returns with a sliding movement into fifth position, accentuating the turnout of the position. On 2 &, the position is held, etc.

On two concluding chords the arm is lowered from second position into preparatory position, the head is turned to the right.

Remarks In battement tendu the working leg is turned out to the utmost in the hip-, knee- and ankle-joints with the knee fully stretched. It moves forcefully out of and into the position. The leg is drawn, in all directions, in an exact straight line, fixing the position of the toe opposite the heel of the supporting leg. The supporting leg is tensed and turned out. The torso is 'pulled up' and calm, keeping the shoulders and hips level, particularly when executing battement tendu to the front and to the back.

The time signature is 2/4. The character of the musical accompaniment is sharp, brisk.

At first battement tendu is executed on two bars, as described, then, according to the degree of accomplishment, on one bar; later on a quarter, beginning the movement on the upbeat; finishing on the quarter in fifth position.

The position sur le cou-de-pied
Sur le cou-de-pied is a position of the working leg on the ankle of

the supporting leg, in front or at the back. This position is utilised in a number of exercises in classical dance.

Sur le cou-de-pied devant The foot of the working leg, with the instep forcefully stretched, grasps the ankle of the supporting leg in such a manner that the heel is located in front and the forcefully stretched toes are drawn to the back.

Sur le cou-de-pied derrière The foot of the working leg touches the ankle of the supporting leg at the back with the heel, the forcefully stretched instep and toes remain in the air.

These are the basic sur le cou-de-pied positions, although in a number of exercises the position sur le cou-de-pied devant appears in a different form: the foot is placed in front so that only the forcefully stretched toes touch the ankle of the supporting leg in front. Such a position sur le cou-de-pied devant is called conditional cou-de-pied. Sur le cou-de-pied derrière is not changed (fig. 9).

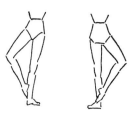

fig. 9   Sur le cou-de-pied positions

The position sur le cou-de-pied is consolidated in a number of exercises.

Example 1 The initial position is fifth position, facing the barre, right leg in front.

On 1 &, the working leg is stretched to second position according to the rules for battement tendu. On 2 &, the leg, bending, is placed with the foot sur le cou-de-pied devant; simultaneously, the turnout of the entire leg is increased. On 3 &, the leg is opened to second position with the toe on the floor. On 4 &, the exercise is concluded in fifth position behind. From here the working leg is stretched to second position, the toe on the floor and, bending the knee, the foot is placed sur le cou-de-pied derrière, touching the supporting leg only with the heel. After that the leg is stretched to second position, the toe on the floor, and the exercise is concluded in fifth position in front.

The exercise is repeated, alternating sur le cou-de-pied devant and derrière.

Example 2 The initial position is fifth position facing the barre, right leg in front. On 1 &, the working leg, bending, is raised to the conditional sur le cou-de-pied devant. Simultaneously, the turnout of the entire leg is increased; on 2 &, the conditional sur le cou-de-pied is held. On 3 &, the working leg is lowered to fifth position. On 4 &, the fifth position is held. On 1 & of the following bar, the left leg is raised sur le cou-de-pied derrière. On 2 &, the position is held etc.

Remarks The given examples are not compulsory: any variant can be used. The given examples consolidate the sur le cou-de-pied positions and are a preparation for a number of exercises of the classical dance.

During the execution of the exercise, the working leg is turned out to the utmost. The supporting leg is taut and turned out. The torso is 'pulled up' and at ease. The working leg in sur le cou-de-pied position preserves its independence. It is particularly important to observe this in sur le cou-de-pied devant, as the foot of the working leg forcefully grasps the ankle of the suppporting leg.

The time signature is 4/4. At first the exercise is executed in two bars, once it has been mastered in one bar. The character of the musical accompaniment is smooth and calm.

Rond de jambe par terre en dehors and en dedans

Ronds de jambe par terre en dehors and en dedans are circles described with the working leg on the floor, outwards and inwards.

Rond de jambe par terre is one of the basic exercises developing the turnout, resilience and mobility of the hip joint. Before studying rond de jambe par terre the concepts en dehors and en dedans are explained.

En dehors, the working leg stretched to the front draws a

semicircle with the toe on the floor, passing through second position to the back, so to speak sliding with the toe outwards, away from the supporting leg.

En dedans, the working leg, stretched to the back, draws a semicircle with the toe on the floor passing through second position to the front, so to speak, inwards, towards the supporting leg.

Rond de jambe par terre en dehors and en dedans are studied after mastering demi rond de jambe par terre. At first rond de jambe par terre is executed in a slow tempo, fixing each direction. Later on, without stops, smoothly combining rond de jambe par terre with passé par terre.

Rond de jambe par terre en dehors The initial position is first position. On 1 &, the working leg is stretched forward according to the rules for battement tendu. On 2 & 3 &, it draws an arc with the toe on the floor, passing through second position and going to the back; the turnout of the entire leg is simultaneously increased, the shoulders and the hips remaining level. On 4 &, without pausing, the leg is drawn with a sliding movement through first position (passé) and on 1 & of the following bar, it is stretched forward. The movement is repeated the required number of times, concluding it in first position.

Rond de jambe par terre en dedans The initial position is first position. On 1&, the working leg is stretched backwards according to the rules for battement tendu. On 2 & 3 &, it draws an arc with the toe on the floor through second position to the front; the turnout of the entire leg is increased while doing this, the shoulders and the hips remain level. On 4&, without pausing, the leg is drawn with a sliding movement through first position (passé) and on 1 & of the following bar it is stretched backwards. The movement is repeated the required number of times, concluding it in first position.

Remarks The 'pull up' and ease of the torso, the stability of the shoulders and the hips, the utmost turnout and tautness of both legs in rond de jambe par terre, facilitate the development of the turnout and the resilience of the hip joint.

The character of the musical accompaniment is smooth, legato. At first the time signature is 4/4, the exercise is executed in one bar. Later on, in one bar of 2/4, but the movement is always executed evenly.

Battement tendu jeté

Battements tendus jetés are stretched movements with a swing. They cultivate the tautness of the legs in the air, develop the strength and lightness of the legs and the mobility of the hip joint (fig. 10).

Battement tendu jeté is studied initially from first position; later on from fifth. After mastering the movement facing the barre, it is executed holding the barre with one hand.

fig. 10
Battement
tendu jeté

Battement tendu jeté to the side The initial position is fifth position, right leg in front, the left hand rests upon the barre, the right arm is in the preparatory position and the head is turned to the right. On two introductory chords, the right arm is opened to second position. On 1 &, the working leg (simultaneously turning the head en face) is thrown with a brush to the side, in second position, at the height of 25°. On 2 &, the working leg is closed in fifth position in front, also with a brush. The stretched instep is not released until the pointed toes have touched the floor and are returning to the initial position, accentuating the turnout of the fifth position. The movement is repeated, alternating fifth position in front and at the back.

Battement tendu jeté to the front The initial position is as described above. On 1 &, the working leg, keeping the hips level, is thrown with a brush to the front, at the height of 25°. On 2 &, the working leg is closed in the initial position also with a brush; the pointed toes, after touching the floor, return into fifth position, accentuating the turnout.

Battement tendu jeté to the back The initial position is fifth position, right leg behind. On 1 &, the working leg is thrown to the back with a brush, at the height of 25°. On 2 &, it returns to the initial position, also with a brush. The stretched instep is only released when the pointed toes touch the floor and the leg returns to fifth position, accentuating the turnout of the heel in fifth position. On two concluding chords, the right arm returns to the preparatory position. The head is turned to the right.

Remarks In battement tendu jeté in all directions, the leg is thrown exactly in a straight line, always establishing the same height in the air. Both legs constantly sustain their turnout and tautness, especially at the moment of the brush. The torso is 'pulled up' and easy, the shoulders and hips are level, especially during battement tendu jeté to the front and to the back.

The time signature is 2/4. The character of the musical accompaniment is very clear-cut and vigorous.

Battement tendu jeté is executed in the same tempo as battement tendu.

Battement tendu pour le pied

This exercise develops the strength and resilience of the instep. At first it is studied facing the barre, from first and then from fifth position. There are two variants of the exercise: lowering the heel to the floor, or flexing the instep of the raised working leg. The second variant is studied only after mastering battement tendu jeté.

1. The initial position is first position. On 1 &, the working leg is stretched to the side according to the rules for battement tendu, so that the toe is located opposite the heel of the supporting leg. On 2 &, the heel of the working leg is lowered to the floor with a strong, but not sharp, movement. On 3 &, the heel is raised from the floor with a forceful movement, lifting it as high as possible, thus stretching the instep. On 4 &, the movement is concluded in the initial position, according to the rules for battement tendu.

Remarks During the movements the legs should be taut and turned out. The torso is 'pulled up'. When the heel is lowered, the centre of the body weight is in no way transferred from the supporting leg to the working leg. After mastering the movement, the heel is lowered to the floor twice in succession or more, keeping the body easy and 'pulled up'.

The time signature and its character are the same as in battement tendu.

2. The initial position is fifth position. On 1 &, the working leg is thrown to the side with a brush, to a height of 25°, according to

the rules for battement tendu jeté. On 2 &, the toe of the working leg is raised to the utmost, shortening the instep; the knee is stretched and the leg maintains its assumed position. On 3 &, the toe is lowered with a forceful movement, stretching the instep; the position of the leg is not changed. On 4 &, the movement is concluded in fifth position behind, according to the rules for battement tendu jeté. The exercise is continued, alternating fifth position in front and behind (fig 11).

fig. 11
Battement tendu
pour le pied

Remarks During the movement both legs are turned out to the utmost. The supporting leg is taut. The torso is 'pulled up' and easy, the shoulders and hips are level. After mastering the movement, it is executed twice in succession, or more.

The time signature and character of the musical accompaniment are the same as in battement tendu jeté.

Battement frappé

Battement frappé is a beating movement. It develops the strength of the leg and the agility and mobility of the knee.

Battement frappé is studied, facing the barre, at first to the side then to the front and to the back. At first in battement frappé, the working leg, stretching in any direction, is opened quickly, sliding with the toe along the floor. After mastering the movement, it is executed holding the barre with one hand: at first with the toe on the floor, after that at a height of 45°.

The initial position is fifth position right leg in front. Préparation is on two introductory chords. On 1, the right arm, opening on the upbeat, is raised through the preparatory position into first position, the head is slightly inclined towards the left shoulder and the eyes are directed towards the hand. On &, the position is held. On 2, the working leg is stretched to the side with the toe on the floor, according to the rules for battement tendu; the right arm is opened in second position, the head is turned to the right. On &, the position is held.

Battement frappé to the front On 1, simultaneously turning the head en face, the working leg is bent, increasing the turnout, and grasps the ankle with a light beat (sur le cou-de-pied devant). On 2, the position is held. On 3, the working leg, maintaining the turnout of the thighs, is forcefully thrust forward at a height of 45°. On 4, the position is held and battement frappé to the front is repeated.

Battement frappé to the side On 1, the working leg is bent, increasing the turnout and, with a light beat, it clasps the ankle (sur le cou-de-pied devant). On 2, the position is held. On 3, the working leg is forcefully thrust to the side at a height of 45°. On 4, the position is held. The movement is repeated alternating sur le cou-de-pied devant and derrière.

Battement frappé to the back On 1, the working leg is bent and, with a light beat, is placed sur le cou-de-pied derrière. On 2, the position is held. On 3, the working leg, increasing the turnout of the upper part, is forcefully thrust to the back, at a height of 45°. During this the shoulders and hips remain level. On 4, the position is held and battement frappé to the back is repeated. On 2 concluding chords, the exercise is ended in fifth position behind, the right arm is lowered into the preparatory position and the head is turned to the right.

Remarks In battement frappé in all directions, the beat of the leg (the accent) is in the air; during this the torso is at ease and 'pulled up', the shoulders and hips are level, and the supporting leg is taut and turned out to the utmost.

At first battement frappé is studied separately, at least eight times in each direction. When this has been mastered, it is executed in all directions, at least four times in each direction.

In the beginning the time signature is 4/4. The exercise is executed in one bar as indicated. Later on the time signature is 2/4. The exercise is executed in one beat, beginning the battement frappé on the upbeat.

> *Example* On the upbeat, the leg is placed sur le cou-de-pied; on 1, it is stretched in the given direction. The position is held etc. Later on battement frappé is executed on each quarter of a bar, accentuating the position in the air at 45°. The character of the musical accompaniment is staccato.

Relevé on demi-point

Relevé is a rise; relevé on demi-point is a rise on half toe. Relevé on demi-point develops the strength of the legs and serves as a preparation for the execution of exercises on demi-point in the subsequent classes. Relevés on demi-point are studied facing the barre, in first, second and fifth positions.

The initial position is first position. The hands are resting lightly upon the barre. The torso is 'pulled up', the knees are forcefully stretched. On 1 & 2 &, the heels gradually leave the floor, the instep is stretched while the legs maintain their turnout and tautness. One should rise as high as possible, increasing the 'pull up' of the torso. On 3 & 4 &, the first position on demi-point is held. On 1 & 2 & of the following bar, the heels are gradually lowered onto the floor, keeping the legs taut and turned out, and relevé is concluded in first position, with the head turned to the right. On 3 & 4 &, the first position is held. In relevé on demi-point in second position the weight of the body is centred evenly over both legs.

In relevé on demi-point in fifth position, the legs are turned out to the utmost and are pressed firmly one against the other (fig. 12).

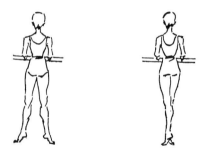

fig. 12   Relevé on demi-point

Remarks In relevés on demi-point in all positions, the feet are placed evenly on the floor; it is not allowed to put the weight on the big toe.

Au milieu, relevé on demi-point is executed following the same rules. The arms can assume various positions, which must be correctly shaped.

The time signature is 4/4. The movement is executed in two bars. After a while, the slow rise on demi-point is alternated with a fast one: on two quarters one rises on demi-point, and on two quarters one returns to the initial position. After mastering relevé on demi-point, it is occasionally combined with demi plié in one and the same exercise.

Petit battement

Petits battements – little beats – develop the mobility and speed of the knee. Petit battement is at first executed facing the barre, later on holding the barre with one hand.

The initial position is fifth position, right leg in front. Préparation: on 1, the right arm, opening on the upbeat, is raised in first position, passing through the preparatory position; the head is inclined slightly towards the left shoulder, the eyes are directed towards the right hand. On &, the right arm is opened to second position, the head is turned to the right, the working leg is stretched in second position according to the rules for battement tendu. On 2, the right leg, increasing the turnout, is bent and placed sur le cou-de-pied devant, the arm remaining in second position. On &, the working leg, simultaneously turning the head en face, is slightly opened in the direction of second position. On 1, the leg, while bending, is placed sur le cou-de-pied derrière. On &, it unbends again in the direction of second position and on 2, it is bent sur le cou-de-pied devant.

Petit battement is executed evenly, alternating sur le cou-de-pied devant and derrière, until the end of the musical phrase (in this case no less than eight bars of 2/4). At the end of the exercise, on the first concluding chord, the working leg is opened in second position with the toe on the floor; on the second chord, it is closed in fifth position behind, the arm is lowered into preparatory position and the head is turned to the right.

Remarks In petit battement the upper part of the working leg, from the hip to the knee, is particularly turned out and immobile; the lower part, from the knee to the toe, accentuates, as it bends and unbends, the sur le cou-de-pied positions devant and derrière. The instep and the toes are forcefully stretched. The supporting leg is taut and turned out. The torso is pulled up and easy. Both arms maintain their assumed positions.

The time signature is 2/4. The character of the musical accompaniment is staccato. At first each movement is executed in one bar: on &, the working leg is unbent; on 1, it is bent; on & 2, the position is held; on &, the leg is unbent, etc. Such a rhythm helps to master correctly the sur le cou-de-pied devant and derrière positions. Later on petit battement is executed on each 1/4 bar, evenly. Once this exercise has been mastered, one can alternate petits battements with pauses with continuous petits battements.

Grand plié

Grand plié, like demi plié, develops the strength and resilience of the leg muscles.

At first grand plié is studied facing the barre, in first position. On the first bar, the legs, following the rules for demi plié, bend as much as possible while keeping the heels on the floor; the heels then gradually leave the floor. The plié continues to its deepest possible point with an increased turnout of both legs, keeping the torso straight and 'pulled up'.

On the second bar, without delay and increasing the turnout, the legs start to straighten slowly, without losing the tension of the muscles; the 'pull up' of the torso is increased. The heels are lowered as soon as possible to the floor, and grand plié is concluded, via demi plié, in the initial position.

Remarks Grand plié is studied in the following order. First, second, third, fifth position and, being the most difficult, fourth position as the last one.

In grand plié in second and fourth positions, the weight of the body is distributed evenly over both legs. In second position the heels are not raised; in all other positions they are raised and lowered evenly, without jerking. It is important to keep them on the floor as long as possible and to lower them again as soon as possible. The feet are placed evenly on the floor; it is not allowed to put the weight on the big toe.

After mastering grand plié facing the barre, it is executed holding the barre with one hand. The initial position is first position, the left hand is resting lightly upon the barre, the right arm is in the preparatory position, the head is turned to the right. On two introductory chords, the right arm is opened to second position. At the beginning of grand plié, the right arm and the head, while turned to the right, are lowered, the eyes follow the hand. When the legs reach the deepest point, the arm is in the preparatory position. When the legs return via demi plié, the arm is raised in first position, the head is inclined to the left, the eyes are directed towards the hand. At the conclusion of grand plié, the arm is opened in second position, the head is turned to the right, the eyes follow the hand.

The changing of the positions in grand plié is done by means of battement tendu: at first on two chords, afterwards on the upbeat, before the following grand plié.

Grand plié is executed au milieu according to the same rules. Both arms accompany the movement in all positions, excluding fourth position, where the arms remain in their initial position (fig. 13).

fig. 13   Grand plié

The time signature is 4/4. The character of the musical accompaniment is legato.

In its final form, the exercise is executed in one bar of 4/4. On the first and second quarters, the legs are bent; on the third and fourth, the legs are straightened.

Battement fondu

Battements fondus are melting, flowing battements. They are more complicated than the previous exercises. They develop the resilience and strength of the legs, imparting softness and flow to the movements.

In the beginning, battement fondu is studied facing the barre: first to the side and then to the back; battement fondu to the front is studied holding the barre with one hand. At first battement fondu is studied with the toe on the floor, and – once it has been mastered – opening the leg at the height of 45°.

Battement fondu to the front Initial position: fifth position right leg in front, the left hand is on the barre, the right arm is in the preparatory position, the head is turned to the right.

Préparation: on two introductory chords. The right arm is opened in second position, the right leg is stretched to the side with the toe on the floor.

On 1 &, both legs are bent gradually, increasing the turnout: the working leg in the direction of the conditional sur le cou-de-pied, the supporting leg beginning demi plié. On 2 &, the working leg assumes the conditional cou-de-pied position, the supporting leg reaches the deepest possible point in demi plié; the torso remains straight and 'pulled up'. On 3 & 4 &, both legs, without delay, are gradually straightened, maintaining the turnout, while the working leg is opened to the front at a height of 45°. Battement fondu to the front is repeated (fig. 14).

fig. 14   Battement fondu

Battement fondu to the side On 1&, both legs are bent gradually, increasing the turnout: the working leg in the direction of the conditional sur le cou-de-pied, the supporting leg beginning demi-plié. On 2 &, the working leg assumes the conditional cou-de-pied position, the supporting leg reaches the deepest possible point in demi plié. On 3 & 4 &, both legs are gradually straightened, maintaining the turnout, while the working leg is opened to the side at 45°. Battement fondu is repeated, but now the working leg is bent in the direction of sur le cou-de-pied derrière and, concluding the movement, it is opened again to the

31

side, at 45°. Battement fondu, when it is repeated, will alternate sur le cou-de-pied devant and derrière.

Battement fondu to the back On 1 &, both legs are bent gradually, increasing the turnout: the working leg in the direction of sur le cou-de-pied derrière, the supporting leg beginning demi-plié. On 2 &, the working leg assumes the sur le cou-de-pied derrière position, the supporting leg reaches the deepest possible point in demi plié. On 3 & 4 &, both legs are gradually straightened, while the working leg, increasing the turnout of the upper part and without disturbing the level of the hips, is opened to the back at 45°. On two concluding chords, battement fondu is ended in fifth position behind, the right arm is lowered in preparatory position, the head is turned to the right.

Remarks At first battement fondu is studied in each direction separately, not more than four consecutive times. After that, one proceeds to battement fondu in all directions, but not less than twice in each direction.

Later on, when executing battement fondu, arm movements are included. At the beginning of battement fondu the right arm is gradually lowered, coming to preparatory position at the moment of demi plié. The head, while turned to the right, is slightly lowered, the eyes following the hand. At the conclusion of battement fondu, the right arm also is opened gradually through first position (the head is inclined to the left) to second position (the head is turned to the right).

After mastering battement fondu it is executed immediately from fifth position; during the demi plié of the supporting leg, the working leg is raised to the conditional cou-de-pied position; the right arm, slightly opening on the upbeat, is then opened through the preparatory and first positions into second position as the working leg, concluding the movement, is opened at 45°.

As a rule the arm movement is executed at the beginning of the exercise, and sometimes in the middle.

Battements fondus should be combined with battements frappés: the smooth, soft battements fondus and the sharp accentuated battements frappés train the muscles for contrasts in movement.

The time signature is 4/4. The character of the musical

accompaniment is legato. Battements fondus are evenly executed, in one bar. Combining them with battements frappés the general line of the melody should be preserved, with only the rhythmical design within the bar marking the difference in character between both movements.

Battement tendu jeté piqué

Battements tendus jetés piqués are pricking movements. They exercise the independent and free movements of the leg in a stretched position.

Initial position: fifth position.

On &, the working leg is thrown to the side with a brushing movement at a height of 25°; on 1, without delay, it touches the floor as if pricking it with the toe (piqué) and flies up to the same height again. On &, the position is held and on 2, it is closed with a brushing movement into fifth position.

Battement tendu jeté piqué is studied in all directions, gradually increasing the number of piqués. Later on, battement tendu jeté piqué is alternated with battement tendu jeté.

Remarks The working leg in the battement tendu jeté piqué is taut and independent, the supporting leg is taut, the torso is 'pulled up' and easy.

The time signature and the character of the musical accompaniment are the same as in battement tendu jeté

Temps relevé par terre

Temps relevé par terre is an exercise which can be utilised as a preparation for rond de jambe par terre en dehors and en dedans.

Temps relevé par terre en dehors Initial position: first position.

On 1, demi plié in first position; the right arm, opening on the upbeat, is closed into preparatory position. On &, the working leg (without delay) is stretched to the front with a sliding movement, the right arm is raised to first position, the head is inclined slightly towards the left shoulder. On 2, the working leg, maintaining the turnout, and sliding with the toe along the floor, describes an arc to the side; the supporting leg is straightened, the right arm is opened to second position, the head is turned to the right. On &, the position is held. After that, temps relevé par terre en dehors is repeated (fig. 15).

Temps relevé par terre en dedans Initial position: first position.

On 1, demi plié in first position; the right arm, opening on the upbeat, is closed into preparatory position. On &, the working leg is stretched to the back with a sliding movement, the right arm is raised to first position, the head is inclined slightly towards the left shoulder. On 2 the working leg (increasing the turnout), sliding with the toe along the floor, describes an arc to the side; the supporting leg is straightened, the right arm is opened to second position, the head is turned to the right. On &, the position is held. After that, temps relevé par terre en dedans is repeated (fig. 16).

fig. 15   *Temps relevé par terre en dehors*   fig. 16   *Temps relevé par terre en dedans*

Later on, the final '&' in temps relevé par terre serves as the upbeat in order to begin rond de jambe par terre. In this case the working leg starting rond de jambe par terre en dehors slides with the toe along the floor from second position to the back. Starting rond de jambe par terre en dedans it slides from second position to the front. By the end of the year temps relevé par terre is executed with rond de jambe par terre at the beginning and in the middle of the exercise.

The time signature is 4/4. The character of the musical accompaniment is the same as in rond de jambe par terre.

Battement double frappé

In battement double frappé, a movement with a double beat, petit battement and battement frappé are combined. It is executed according to the rules for these exercises. It develops the agility and mobility of the legs.

Initial position: fifth position; the préparation is the same as the one for battement frappé.

On 1, the working leg is bent grasping the ankle (sur le cou-de-pied devant). On & 2, it is placed sur le cou-de-pied derrière, according to the rules for petit battement. On & 3, the leg is stretched to the side with the toe on the floor, according to the rules for battement frappé. On & 4, the position is held. On & 1, the leg is bent and placed sur le cou-de-pied derrière. On & 2, it is brought sur le cou-de-pied devant. On & 3, it is stretched to the side with the toe on the floor. On & 4, the position is held, etc. After mastering battement double frappé to the side, one proceeds to the study of battement double frappé in all directions. From second position the leg is bent and placed sur le cou-de-pied derrière, then brought sur le cou-de-pied devant and stretched to the front.

As it is again bent, it is now placed sur le cou-de-pied devant, brought sur le cou-de-pied derrière and stretched to the side. Again it is placed sur le cou-de-pied devant, brought sur le cou-de-pied derrière and stretched to the back. Now it is bent sur le cou-de-pied derrière, is brought sur le cou-de-pied devant and is then stretched to the side etc.

Battement double frappé is executed in any direction and in various combinations.

Remarks While executing battement double frappé, especially en croix, the torso remains completely at ease and 'pulled up', the supporting leg is taut and turned out, the upper part of the working leg is turned out and immobile.

After mastering battement double frappé with the toe on the floor, one proceeds to study battement double frappé with the leg opening at a height of 45°. The rules are the same as those for battement frappé at 45°.

At first the time signature is 2/4. The character of the musical accompaniment is staccato. Battement double frappé is executed in two bars, later on in one bar. In the first case the movements are executed on eighths, the fourth 1/8 is a pause; later on the movement is begun on the upbeat and executed in 1/4.

Battement relevé lent at 90°

Battement relevé lent is a slow raising of the leg at 90°. It develops the strength and lightness of the legs at the required height.

Battement relevé lent at 90° to the front Initial position: fifth position.

On two introductory chords the right arm, opening on the upbeat, is opened to second position. The working leg is

fig. 17   Battement relevé lent at 90° to the front

stretched to the front with a sliding movement and without delaying it on the floor it is slowly raised, exactly in a straight line, to a height of 90°. Both legs are taut and turned out, the torso is 'pulled up'. The taut working leg is established at the required height and is then slowly lowered. Touching the floor with stretched toes, it returns with a sliding movement to fifth position (fig. 17).

Battement relevé lent at 90° to the side With a sliding movement

fig. 18   Battement relevé lent at 90° to the side

the working leg is stretched to the side with the toe on the floor and, without delay and maintaining the exact direction of second position, it is raised slowly to a height of 90°. The taut and turned out leg is established at the required height, after which it is lowered slowly and, touching the floor with stretched toes, returns with a sliding movement to fifth position (fig. 18). Battement relevé lent to the side is repeated closing alternately in fifth position in front or behind.

Battement relevé lent at 90° to the back With a sliding movement the working leg is stretched to the back and, without delaying it on the floor it is slowly raised to a height of 90°, exactly in a straight line. The leg is turned out and taut. The torso, keeping the hips and shoulders level, is directed slightly forward. After establishing the required height, the working leg slowly starts to lower. The torso is brought upright, returning to its initial position at the conclusion of the battement relevé lent in fifth position

fig. 19   Battement relevé lent at 90° to the back

(fig. 19). On two concluding chords, the right arm is lowered in preparatory position and the head is turned to the right.

Remarks Battement relevé lent is at first studied to the side, facing the barre. After that, to the back, in the same manner. Battement relevé lent to the front is studied, later on, holding the barre with one hand. At first, battement relevé lent is executed separately, at least four times in each direction; later on at least twice consecutively in all directions.

It is imperative to watch that both arms, the one on the barre and the one in second position, are accurately held, as their correct position tends not be sustained, particularly in battement relevé lent to the back. The supporting leg preserves its tautness and turnout. The torso is 'pulled up', particularly with regard to its inevitable forward inclination in battement relevé lent to the back.

At first the head remains in the en face position; later on battement relevé lent to the front and to the back are executed with the head turned towards the side of the working leg. In battement relevé lent to the side, the head remains en face. The working leg may be raised above 90° if the physical ability of the pupil allows this.

The time signature is 4/4. The character of the musical accompaniment is legato. The exercise is executed in two bars: for 3/4 of the first bar the leg is raised; on the fourth 1/4 and on the first 1/4 of the second bar, the leg is fixed at the required height. For the remaining 3/4 of the second bar, the leg is lowered to fifth position. When a 3/4 time is utilised, the exercise is executed in eight bars. For three bars – raising the leg; on the

37

fourth and fifth bars, fixing the height; and for three bars returning to the initial position.

Rond de jambe en l'air

Ronds de jambe en l'air are circular movements of the leg in the air, they cultivate the agility and mobility of the leg from the knee to the toes. This exercise, like rond de jambe par terre, is executed en dehors and en dedans.

Preparatory exercise for rond de jambe en l'air Initial position: fifth position right leg in front, the torso is 'pulled up', the hands rest lightly upon the barre.

On the first introductory chord the position is held; on the second the working leg is stretched to the side with the toe on the floor. On 1 &, the working leg, taut and turned out, is raised to a height of 45°. On 2 &, increasing the turnout, it is bent, directing the toe to the middle of the calf of the working leg. On 3 &, the working leg, without disturbing the turnout or the height of 45°, is stretched to second position, and on 4 & it is lowered on to the floor with stretched toes. The exercise is repeated from four to eight times, ending in fifth position behind on two concluding chords.

At first rond de jambe en l'air is studied facing the barre; later on, holding the barre with one hand.

Rond de jambe en l'air en dehors Initial position: fifth position right leg in front.

Two introductory chords. On 1, the right arm (opening on the upbeat) is raised to first position; the head inclines slightly towards the left shoulder, the eyes are directed towards the hand. On &, the working leg is stretched to second position with the toe on the floor, the right arm is opened to second position and the head is turned to the right. On 2, the working leg is raised in second position, at a height of 45°, and the head is turned en face.

On 1 &, the working leg, with the upper part completely immobile, is bent at the knee. Holding the turnout of the heel, it describes an arc en dehors, a little to the back, as the pointed toe is directed to the middle of the calf. On 2 &, the working leg, increasing the turnout of the heel, extends, describing an arc, a little forward, concluding the movement of the utmost taut and turned out leg in second position, at a height of 45°. On 3 & 4, the position is held (fig. 20).

Rond de jambe en l'air en dedans
Initial position: fifth position right leg behind. On two introductory chords the right leg is raised at 45°, the head is turned en face.

On 1 &, the working leg, with the upper part completely immobile, is bent at the knee. Increasing the turn-

fig. 20   Rond de jambe en l'air en dehors

out of the heel, it describes an arc en dedans, a little forward, directing the stretched toe to the middle of the calf. On 2 &, the working leg being stretched describes an arc a little to the back, concluding the movement of the utmost taut and turned out working leg in second position, at a height of 45°. On 3 & 4 the position is held (fig. 21).

Remarks In rond de jambe en l'air the body weight is centred over the supporting leg. The turnout and the immobility of the upper part of the working leg develops the ability of the knee to make circular movements, cultivating the agility and mobility of the lower leg. The supporting leg is as taut and turned out as possible. Both arms, the one on the barre and the one in second position maintain the correct position.

fig. 21   Rond de jambe en l'air en dedans

The time signature is 4/4. The character of the musical accompaniment is smooth but clear. At first rond de jambe en l'air is studied in one bar. After that, in one 2/4 bar, beginning on the upbeat. For example: starting the circle on &, it is concluded on 1, holding the position at 45° on & 2; on & 3, the following circle is started, continuing the movements in this way to the end of the musical phrase.

Battement soutenu
Battement soutenu is a sustained movement. It develops the

resilience and the turnout of the legs.

Battement soutenu to the front Initial position: fifth position. On two introductory chords the right arm is opened to second position.

On the upbeat, on &, the working leg (simultaneously turning the head en face) is raised to the conditional cou-de-pied position; on 1 &, it begins (increasing the turnout) to stretch to the front, as the supporting leg begins demi plié. On 2 &, the working leg, continuing the movement, slides with pointed toes forward along the floor, as the supporting leg continues demi plié. On 3 &, the taut and turned out working leg returns, drawing the toe along the floor, towards fifth position, as the supporting leg begins to straighten; on 4, both legs are straightened in a tight fifth position.

Battement soutenu to the side Initial position: fifth position.

On the upbeat, on &, the working leg is raised to the conditional cou-de-pied position; on 1 &, it begins (increasing the turnout) to stretch to the side as the supporting leg begins demi plié; on 2 &, the working leg, continuing the movement, slides with pointed toes sideways along the floor, as the supporting leg continues demi plié. On 3 &, the taut and turned out working leg returns towards fifth position in front, drawing the toe along the floor, as the supporting leg begins to straighten; on 4, both legs are straightened in a tight fifth position. Battement soutenu is repeated once again, ending in fifth position behind.

Battement soutenu to the back On the upbeat, on &, the working leg is raised sur le cou-de-pied derrière; on 1 & it begins (increasing turnout) to stretch to the back as the supporting leg begins demi plié, the shoulders and hips remaining level. On 2 &, the working leg, continuing the movement, slides with pointed toes along the floor to the back as the supporting leg continues demi plié. The torso, maintaining the 'pull up', is directed slightly forward. On 3 &, the taut and turned out working leg, drawing the toe along the floor, returns towards fifth position as the supporting leg begins to straighten; on 4 &, both legs are straightened in a tight fifth position. On two concluding chords the right arm is lowered in preparatory position as the head is turned to the right.

After mastering relevé on demi-point battement soutenu is executed with a rise on demi-point in fifth position.

Initial position: fifth position right leg in front. We have 3/8 in the anacrusis. On the first 1/8 the arm is opened slightly, on the second 1/8 it is lowered in preparatory position simultaneously with the rise on demi-point in fifth position. On the third 1/8 the arm is raised in first position, the head is inclined towards the left shoulder, the working leg is raised in the conditional cou-de-pied position.

On 1 &, the suppporting leg, lowering the heel to the floor, begins demi plié; the working leg is gradually stretched forward with the toe on the floor. The arm is opened in second position, the head is turned to the right. On 2 &, the working leg, continuing the movement, slides forward along the floor with pointed toes, the supporting leg continues demi plié. On 3 &, the working leg begins to return towards fifth position as the supporting leg begins to straighten; both legs are straightened simultaneously in a tight fifth position on demi-point. On 4 &, the position is held. '&' is the upbeat for the next battement soutenu (fig. 22). At the conclusion of the exercise the arm is lowered into the preparatory position as one lowers into fifth position.

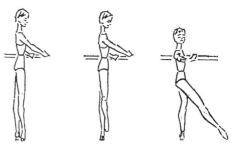

fig. 22   Battement soutenu to the front

Battement soutenu in all directions is executed according to these rules. The supporting leg, coming down from demi-point, must fully maintain its tautness, beginning demi plié only after the heel has touched the floor.

Remarks Especially important in battement soutenu is the flow of the movement: it is executed completely evenly and continuously.

The torso is always 'pulled up'. Both arms, the one on the barre and the one in second position, maintain their correct positions.

At first battement soutenu is executed separately, four times in each direction; after that, no more than twice consecutively to the front, to the side, to the back and to the side. Later on, battement soutenu to the front and to the back is accompanied by a turn of the head towards the arm which is opened in second position. In battement soutenu to the side the head remains en face.

Battement soutenu is combined with exercises like battement fondu, battement frappé and battement double frappé.

The time signature is 4/4. The character of the musical accompaniment is legato. The movement is executed in one bar.

Grand battement jeté

Grand battement jeté is a large, swinging movement. Like battement relevé lent at 90°, it develops strength and lightness and improves the height of the legs.

Grand battement jeté to the front Initial position: fifth position. The torso is 'pulled up' and easy, the legs are 'pulled up' and turned out, the right arm is opened in second position.

On 1, the working leg is lightly thrown forward with a brushing movement, exactly on a straight line, at a height of at least 90°. On &, the taut and turned out leg, sustaining the tension of the muscles, is lowered to the floor with pointed toes. On 2, it returns with a sliding movement into fifth position. On &, the initial position is held.

Grand battement jeté to the side On 1 the working leg is lightly thrown to the side with a brushing movement, exactly in a straight line at a height of at least 90°. On &, the taut and turned out leg, sustaining the tension of the muscles, is lowered to the floor with pointed toes. On 2, it is returned with a sliding movement into fifth position. On &, the initial position is held. Grand battement jeté to the side is repeated, alternating fifth position in front and behind.

Grand battement jeté to the back Initial position: fifth position, working leg behind.

On 1, the working leg is lightly thrown to the back, with a

brushing movement, exactly in a straight line, at a height of at least 90°. The torso, increasing the 'pull up', is directed slightly forward. The shoulders and hips remain level. On &, the taut and turned out working leg, sustaining the tension of the muscles, is lowered to the floor with pointed toes. On 2, it returns with a sliding movement into fifth position; the torso is brought upright, returning to its initial position. On &, the initial position is held. On two concluding chords the arm is lowered in preparatory position as the head is turned to the right.

Remarks The study of grand battement jeté is begun facing the barre. First to the side, then to the back. Grand battement jeté to the front is studied holding the barre with one hand.

At first, grand battement jeté is executed separately, eight times in each direction; afterwards, four consecutive times en croix. It is necessary to observe that both arms, the one in second position and the one on the barre, maintain their correct positions, as they have the tendency to lose them, especially with grand battement jeté to the back. The supporting leg maintains its tautness and turnout all the time, particularly at the moment of the upward swing of the leg. The torso is 'pulled up' and at ease. When swinging the leg to the back, one must resist the unavoidable inclination of the torso, bringing it upright as soon as the leg returns to the initial position. The forceful thrust should not disturb the level of the shoulders and hips. The positions of the head in grand battement jeté are the same as when executing battement relevé lent.

The time signature is 2/4. The character of the musical accompaniment is energetic, brisk. At first grand battement jeté is executed in two bars: one bar – the movement, the second bar – a pause; afterwards the exercise is executed in one bar and, finally on every 1/4, beginning the movement on the upbeat on &.

Battement développé
Battement développé is an unfolding movement; it develops the strength of the legs and the turnout of the hip joint, which is indispensable for the so called 'leg elevation'; it also cultivates the refinement of the basic poses of the classical dance.

Battement développé to the front Initial position: fifth position.

On two introductory chords the right arm, opening on the upbeat, is opened in second position.

On 1&, the working leg, pointing the foot, is raised to the conditional cou-de-pied position. On 2 &, it slides in a continuous movement along the supporting leg and, increasing the turnout, is raised to the middle of the knee of the supporting leg. The torso is 'pulled up'. On 3 & 4, the working leg is stretched to the front at a height of at least 90°, keeping the hips level and increasing the turnout of the heel. On 1 & of the second bar, the taut and turned out leg is fixed at the height of 90°. On 2 & 3, the working leg is lowered slowly, according to the rules for battement relevé lent. On 4, the movement is concluded in fifth position.

Battement développé to the side Initial position: fifth position.

On 1 &, the working leg, pointing the instep and toes, is raised to the conditional cou-de-pied position. On 2 &, it slides, in a continuous movement, along the supporting leg and, increasing the turnout, is raised to the middle of the knee of the supporting leg. The torso is 'pulled up'. On 3 & 4, the working leg, raising the thigh, is gradually stretched to the side at a height of at least 90° sustaining an exact second position. On 1 & of the second bar, the taut and turned out working leg is fixed at the height of 90°. On 2&3, it is slowly lowered according to the rules for battement relevé lent. On 4, the movement is concluded in fifth position in front (fig. 23).

fig. 23   Battement développé to the side

Battement développé to the side is repeated, concluding it in fifth position behind, and is then continued via sur le cou-de-pied derrière. The working leg, pointing the instep and toes, is raised sur le cou-de-pied derrière and slides in a continuous movement along the supporting leg; it is raised to the level of the knee and stretched to the side; after establishing the height of 90°, the working leg is lowered in fifth position in front.

Battement développé to the back Initial position: fifth position, right leg behind.

On 1 &, the working leg, pointing the instep and the toes, is raised sur le cou-de-pied derrière. On 2 &, it slides without interruption along the supporting leg and, increasing the turn-out of the thigh, is raised to the level of the knee of the supporting leg. The torso is 'pulled up'. On 3 & 4, the knee of the working leg is strongly drawn to the back, the upper part is raised as high as possible and it is stretched to the back, exactly along a straight line, not lower than 90°. The torso, increasing the 'pull up', is directed slightly forward. The shoulders and hips remain level.

On 1 & of the following bar, the taut and turned out working leg is fixed at the height of 90°. On 2 & 3, the working leg is slowly lowered according to the rules for battement relevé lent, the torso is brought upright into the initial position, simultaneously with the returning of the leg to fifth position. On two concluding chords, the right arm is lowered into the preparatory position as the head is turned to the right.

Remarks Battement développé to the side and to the back is first studied facing the barre. To the front holding the barre with one hand. At first battement développé is executed four consecutive times in each direction separately. Afterwards, twice consecutively to the front, to the side, to the back and to the side.

In battement développé the working leg is turned out to the utmost, the supporting leg is taut and turned out. The torso is 'pulled up', especially at the moment of its unavoidable inclination when executing battement développé to the back. Both arms, the one in second position and the one on the barre, must be held accurately, avoiding the tendency not to sustain their correct positions. At the beginning of the study the head remains en face. Afterwards battement développé to the front and to the back are executed with a turn of the head towards the working leg. In battement développé to the side the head remains en face.

When beginning to study battement développé, the arm is opened in second position on two introductory chords. On two concluding chords, it is lowered into the preparatory position. Afterwards the arm accompanies the movement: opening on the upbeat it is raised in first position when the leg is raised from fifth position to the knee, the head is inclined slightly towards the left shoulder, the eyes are directed towards the hand; when the leg is stretched the arm is opened in second position and the head is turned to the right. At the conclusion of the exercise the arm is lowered slowly, simultaneously with the leg, into the initial position.

The time signature is 4/4. The character of the musical accompaniment is legato.

Grand battement jeté piqué

Grand battement jeté piqué, a movement with a high, pricking swing, is executed according to the rules for grand battement jeté.

Initial position: fifth position. The movement is started on the upbeat. The taut working leg is thrown from fifth position, with a brushing movement, to a height of not less than 90°. On 1, it is lowered, sustaining the tension of all muscles and touching the floor with the fully pointed toe. It repeats the throw on &; on 2, the working leg is returned with sliding movement into fifth position. The upbeat for the throwing of the leg is &.

Remarks In grand battement jeté in all directions, the toe of the working leg touches the floor at a point opposite the heel of the supporting leg. The supporting leg is taut and turned out at all times, especially at the moment of the upward thrust. The torso is 'pulled up' and at ease. When throwing the leg to the back, one should resist the unavoidable inclination of the torso, bringing it upright as the leg is lowered to the floor. The forceful throwing of the leg should not disturb the level of the shoulders and hips. Both arms, the one in second position and the one on the barre, sustain their correct positions at the moment of the throwing. At first, grand battement jeté piqué is alternated with grand battement jeté; afterwards they are executed several times consecutively in one direction.

The time signature is 2/4 or 4/4. The character of the musical accompaniment is the same as in grand battement jeté.

Rond de jambé soutenu en dehors

Initial position: first position. On the upbeat the arm is opened to the side, the head is turned to the right.

On 1 demi plié in first position, the right arm is lowered into the preparatory position. On &, the working leg is stretched forward with a sliding movement, the right arm is raised in first position, the head is inclined slightly towards the left shoulder, the eyes are directed towards the hand. On 2 &, the working leg, sustaining the turnout, slides along the floor describing an arc to second position; the head is turned to the right, the eyes follow the hand. On 3 &, the working leg, increasing the turnout, continues to draw an arc with the toe on the floor to the back, finishing with the toe opposite the heel of the supporting leg; the 'pulled up' torso is directed slightly forward, the head (which is turned to the right) continues the line of the torso. The supporting leg remains in demi plié all the time. On 4, the supporting leg is straightened, the working leg returns to first position according to the rules for battement tendu, the torso is brought upright, the arm is lowered into the preparatory position and the head is turned to the right.

Rond de jambe en dedans

Initial position: first position. On the upbeat, the right arm is opened to the side, the head is turned to the right.

On 1, demi plié in first position, the right arm is lowered into the preparatory position. On &, the working leg, increasing the turnout, is stretched to the back with a sliding movement, the right arm is raised in first position, the head is inclined slightly towards the left shoulder, the eyes are directed towards the hand. On 2 &, while the torso is 'pulled up', the working leg, increasing the turnout, slides along the floor describing an arc with the toe to second position, the right arm is opened in second position, the head is turned to the right, the eyes follow the hand.

On 3 &, the working leg, increasing the turnout, continues to draw an arc to the front with the toe on the floor. The toe finishes opposite the heel of the supporting leg, the head remains turned to the right, the supporting leg remaining in demi plié all the time. On 4, the supporting leg is straightened, the working leg returns to first position, according to the rules for battement tendu, the right arm is lowered into the preparatory position, the head is turned to the right.

Rond de jambe soutenu is usually executed immediately after rond de jambe par terre.

The character of the musical accompaniment is legato. The time signature is 4/4. At first rond de jambe soutenu is studied in two bars: on 1, demi plié; on 2, the leg is stretched forward; on 3, it slides to the side; on 4, the position is held. On 1 & 2 of the second bar, the leg slides to the back; on 3, the movement is concluded in the initial position; on 4, this position is held. Afterwards rond de jambe soutenu is executed in one bar.

Bends of the torso
Bending the torso sideways and backwards is studied at the conclusion of the exercises, in first position, facing the barre. It is necessary to ensure that the tautness of the legs and the 'pull up' of the pelvis are sustained while bending. Third port de bras also is first studied as an independent exercise, standing at the barre in first position, afterwards it is combined with one of the barre exercises. When executing third port de bras, the hand that rests upon the barre maintains its correct position.

Exercices au milieu

The exercises au milieu are begun from the first lessons onwards, studying the positions of the legs and positions and exercises of the arms. As soon as the pupils acquire a certain degree of stability in the exercises at the barre, these exercises are transferred, in the same order, to the centre of the room. The tempo of the movements remains the same as at the barre.

In the exercises au milieu the arms are opened in second position on two introductory chords, remaining completely free and without strain during the exercise. This maintains the 'pull up' and the freedom of the torso, an important prerequisite for the development of stability in dance. On two concluding chords, or at the end of the musical phrase, the arms are lowered into the preparatory position.

In the exercises au milieu one should gradually include turns of the torso from the en face position to épaulement and vice versa; for this purpose the exercises are combined with the port de bras and poses of the classical dance. The turning of the torso and head coincides with the turn of the legs in fifth position. During the turn, the heels are slightly raised from the floor, the turnout of fifth position is maintained.

In a sequence of exercises executed in series, the second arm position is slightly lowered: the arms are opened to the side from the raised preparatory position. The level of the raised preparatory position is between preparatory position and first position.

Epaulement

In classical dance the use of the frontal (en face) position of the body is seldom sustained. Much more often we come across épaulement positions: this means positions of the body with a particular turn of the shoulders. The necessity of épaulement becomes clear from the first classes, where port de bras and poses are studied. In classical dance there are two kinds of épaulement: épaulement croisé and épaulement effacé. They determine the direction of the majority of the poses and movements. To the extent that in the syllabus for the first class it is the starting position for the exercises au milieu, épaulement croisé is already included in the initial stages of study. Epaulement effacé is allowed as a starting position only after mastering the poses effacé and écarté.

Explaining the épaulement positions to the students, one should make use of the class diagram introduced by A. Vaganova in her book *Basic Principles of Classical Ballet.*

Epaulement croisé In order to transfer the body to the épaulement croisé position, one should direct the torso and the legs in fifth position, right foot

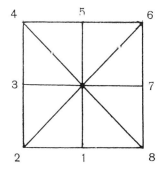

in front, from the en face position towards point 8 of the class diagram, with the head turned to the right. The right shoulder and the right leg are aiming forward, the turn of the head so to speak crosses and sharpens the direction.[1]. The fundamental character of croisé is the crossing of the legs. In épaulement croisé with the left leg the torso and the legs are directed towards point 2 of the class diagram, with the head turned to the left. The arms remain in preparatory position.

Epaulement effacé In order to transfer the body to the épaulement effacé position one should direct the torso and the legs in fifth position, right foot in front, from the en face position towards point 2 of the class diagram, with the head turned to the left. In this position it seems as if the body hides and removes itself from the spectator, the turn of the head to the left softening the contours of the pose[2]. In this position, in contrast with croisé, the legs are open. In épaulement effacé with the left leg the torso and the legs are directed towards point 8 of the class diagram, with the head turned to the right. The arms remain in the preparatory position.

The artistic colouring of épaulement depends on the 'pull up' of the torso, with the shoulders opened and lowered, and on the active turn of the head in profile, with the corresponding eye direction.

The first and second positions are usually directed en face. For the fourth position, épaulement croisé and effacé are characteristic. The third and fifth positions are usually executed in épaulement. When dancing, épaulement and en face positions may be utilised. In order to master épaulement, in the first year, the pupils should sustain it in fifth position for the duration of eight or sixteen bars. The character of the musical accompaniment is legato. The musical beat is 4/4 or 3/4.

Port de bras
After mastering the arm positions and épaulement, one should proceed to study port de bras, which cultivate the arm movements and impart a feeling for co-ordination.

[1] croisé = crossed
[2] effacé = effaced

Preparatory port de bras Initial position: épaulement croisé, fifth position right foot in front.

On 1 & 2 the arms, opening on the upbeat, are raised in first position via the preparatory position, the head is inclined slightly towards the left shoulder, the eyes are directed towards the hands. On 3 & 4 the arms, keeping the shoulders opened and lowered, are opened in second position, the head is turned to the right, the eyes follow the right hand. On 1 & 2 of the second bar the position is held. On 3 & 4, the hands, without changing the level of the arms, are opened and turned with the palms facing downwards, the elbows are softened slightly and the arms are lowered gradually into the preparatory position.[1]

The head remains turned to the right. The port de bras is repeated from two to four times, after which one should execute it with the other leg in front.

After mastering port de bras from the preparatory position, one proceeds to study port de bras from second position. On two introductory chords, the arms are opened via first position into second position. On 1 & 2, the arms are lowered into the preparatory position. On 3 & 4, they are raised in first position; on 1 & 2 of the second bar, concluding the movement, they are opened in second position. On 3 & 4, the position is held.

First port de bras Initial position: fifth position épaulement croisé, right foot in front.

On 1 & 2 the arms, opening on the upbeat, are raised, via the preparatory position, to first position, the head is inclined slightly towards the left shoulder, the eyes are directed towards the hands. On 3 & 4, the arms are raised in third position, the head, turning to the right, is raised slightly, the eyes are directed towards the right hand. On 1 & 2 of the second bar, the arms without losing their curve, and starting the movement at the fingers, are opened in second position; the head is turned to the right, the eyes follow the right hand. On 3 & 4 the hands, without changing the level of the arms, are opened and turned with the palms facing downwards, the elbows are softened slightly and the arms are lowered gradually into the preparatory position. The movement is repeated from two to four times,

---

[1] Later on, when using the words 'the arms are lowered', we always mean in the manner described above.

after which one should execute it with the left foot in front.

Second port de bras Initial position: fifth position, épaulement croisé, right leg in front.

Two introductory chords. On 1 & the arms, opening on the upbeat, are raised through the preparatory position to first position. The head is inclined slightly towards the left shoulder, the eyes are directed towards the hands. On 2 &, the left arm is raised in third position, the right one is opened in second position, the head is turned to the right, the eyes follow the right hand. On 1 & 2 of the first bar, the left arm, starting the movement from the fingers, is opened in second position, the head is turned to the left, the eyes follow the left hand. On 3 & 4 &, the right arm, now being raised, is curved in third position, the left arm, turning the palm of the hand downwards, is lowered into the raised preparatory position. The eyes follow this hand, the head is lowered slightly, turning to the right, the eyes are directed past the elbow of the right arm. On 1 & 2 of the second bar, the right arm is lowered and the left one is raised, so that they meet in first position; the head inclines towards the left shoulder, the eyes are directed towards the hands. On 3 & 4 the left arm is raised in third position, the right one is opened in second position, the head is turned to the right and the movement is concluded in the initial position of second port de bras. From here it is repeated from two to four times, after which, on two concluding chords, on 1 &, the left arm is opened in second position. On 2 &, both arms are lowered in preparatory position (fig. 24).

fig. 24   Second port de bras

Remarks In port de bras the arms move completely freely and independently, while the torso is 'pulled up' and the shoulders are opened and lowered. The movements of the head and the eye direction add to the artistry of the movement.

The character of the musical accompaniment is legato. On a 4/4 time the port de bras is executed in two bars. On a 3/4 time the port de bras is executed in 4 bars.

Third port de bras Initial position: fifth position, épaulement croisé, right leg in front.

Two introductory chords. On 1 &, the arms, opening on the upbeat, are raised through the preparatory position to first position, the head inclines slightly towards the left shoulder, the eyes are directed towards the hands. On 2 &, the arms open in second position, the head turns to the right, the eyes follow the right hand. On 1&2 the torso, increasing the 'pull up' (especially in the pelvic region) bends forward gradually, without losing the tension of the legs or the 'pull up' of the pelvis. Both arms are lowered, meeting in the preparatory position, the head is lowered together with the bend of the torso, the eyes follow the right hand. On 3 & 4, the torso returns gradually to the initial position, the arms are raised through first position to third position, the head turning to the right. On 1 & 2 of the second bar the torso, increasing the 'pull up' (especially in the pelvic region), bends gradually backwards at the waist, starting from the upper back, without losing the tension of the legs and the 'pull up' of the pelvis; the arms maintain an accurate third position, the head remaining turned to the right. On 3 & 4 the torso, after reaching the utmost point of the back-bend, returns gradually to the initial position and the arms open in second position, concluding third port de bras (fig. 25).

The movement is executed the required number of times. On two concluding chords, the arms are lowered into the preparatory position.

The sidebend of the torso Initial position: first position, en face. On two introductory chords the arms are opened in second position.

On 1 & 2 &, the torso, increasing the 'pull up' bends smoothly from the waist to the right without disturbing the level of the

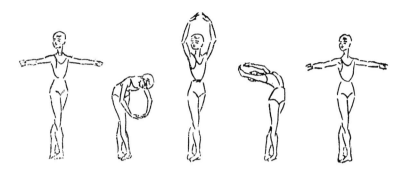

fig. 25   Third port de bras

hips or losing the tension of the legs; while bending, the left arm is raised in third position, the head turns to the right, the right arm remains in second position. On 3 & 4 &, the torso is brought upright smoothly, the left arm opens in second position, the head turns en face. On the following bar the side-bend is repeated to the left etc.

Remarks In all port de bras the legs are kept taut to the utmost, the pelvis and torso are 'pulled up', the shoulders are lowered and opened, the arms and the head, maintaining accurate positions, avoid the slightest tension. It is particularly important to remember these rules when bending forward in third port de bras.

The character of the musical accompaniment is legato. The time signature is 4/4. At first port de bras is executed in two bars, afterwards in one bar. In 3/4 time, port de bras is executed first in eight bars, later in four.

Poses of the classical dance

One proceeds to study the poses of the classical dance after mastering the correct placement of the torso, legs and arms, and having acquired elementary co-ordination of movement. In the first year the poses croisé, effacé and écarté devant and derrière are studied with the toe pointed on the floor. They do not have the same expressiveness we see when the poses of the classical dance are executed with the working leg at a height of 90°.

The poses of the classical dance are as a rule executed from épaulement croisé as the initial position.

Pose croisée devant Initial position: fifth position, épaulement croisé, right leg in front.

On 1 &, the arms, opening on the upbeat, are raised through the preparatory position into first position, the head inclines slightly towards the left shoulder, the eyes are directed towards the hands. On 2 &, the right leg is stretched forward in the direction of point 8 of the class diagram, the left arm is raised in third position, the right arm is opened in second position, the head turns to the right, the eyes following the right hand. On 3 & 4 &, the pose croisée devant is held. On 1 & of the second bar, the left arm is opened in second position and on 2 &, both arms are lowered in preparatory position and the right leg returns to fifth position, according to the rules for battement tendu, concluding the pose in the initial position. On 3 & 4, the initial position is held (fig. 26).

Pose croisée derrière Initial position: fifth position, épaulement croisé, right leg in front.

On 1 &, the arms, opening on the upbeat, are raised through the preparatory position into first position, the head inclines slightly towards the left shoulder, the eyes are directed towards the hands. On 2 &, the left leg is stretched to the back in the direction of point 4 of the class diagram, the left arm is raised in third position, the right one is opened in second position, the head turns to the right, the eyes following the right hand. On 3 & 4, the pose croisée derrière is held. On 1 &, of the second bar, the left arm is opened in second position, on 2 &, both arms are lowered into preparatory position and the left leg returns to fifth position, concluding the pose in the initial position. On 3 & 4 the initial position is held (fig. 27).

Pose effacée devant Initial position: fifth position, épaulement effacé, right leg in front.

On 1 &, the arms, opening on the upbeat, are raised through the preparatory position into first position, the head inclines slightly to the right shoulder, the eyes are directed towards the hands. On 2 &, the right leg is stretched forward in the direction of point 2 of the class diagram, the left arm is raised in third

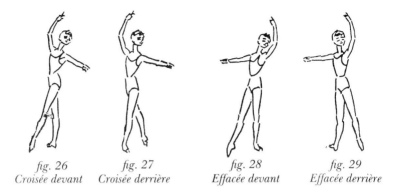

| *fig. 26* | *fig. 27* | *fig. 28* | *fig. 29* |
| Croisée devant | Croisée derrière | Effacée devant | Effacée derrière |

position, the right one is opened in second position, the head turns to the left, the eye direction corresponds with the turn of the head. The torso, increasing the 'pull up' with the hips level and the shoulders opened and lowered, inclines slightly to the back. On 3 & 4, the pose effacée is held. On 1 & of the second bar the left arm is opened in second position; on 2 &, both arms are lowered in preparatory position, the torso is brought upright and the right leg returns to fifth position, concluding the pose in the initial position. On 3 & 4, the position is held (fig. 28).

Pose effacée derrière Initial position: fifth position, épaulement effacé, right leg in front.

On 1 &, the arms, opening on the upbeat, are raised through the preparatory position into first position, the head inclines slightly towards the right shoulder, the eyes are directed towards the hands. On 2 &, the left leg is stretched to the back in the direction of point 6 of the class diagram; the left arm is raised in third position, the right arm is opened in second position; the head, turning to the left, is raised slightly, the glance following the left hand; the torso, increasing the 'pull up', with the hips level and the shoulders opened and lowered, is directed forward, imparting a flying line to the entire figure. On 3 & 4, the pose effacée is held.

On 1 & of the second bar, the left arm is opened in second position, the torso is brought upright, the head turns to the left, the eyes following the hand. On 2 &, both arms are lowered into preparatory position, the left leg returns to fifth position, and the pose is concluded in the initial position. On 3 & 4, the initial position is held (fig. 29).

Pose écartée derrière Pose écartée derrière explains graphically the term écartée, 'put aside'. This is why it is recommended to study it first in this direction.

Initial position: fifth position, épaulement effacé, right leg in front.

On 1 &, the arms, opening on the upbeat, are raised through the preparatory position into the first position; the head inclines slightly towards the right shoulder, the eyes are directed towards the hands. On 2 &, the right leg, increasing the turnout, is stretched in the direction of point 4 of the class diagram, the right arm is raised in third position, the left one is opened in second position, the head turns to the left, the eyes follow the left hand. The torso, increasing the 'pull up', keeping the hips level and the shoulders opened and lowered, is inclined slightly to the left. On 3 & 4 the pose écartée derrière is held, both legs are kept taut and turned out to the utmost.

On 1 & of the second bar, the right arm is opened in second position, the torso is brought upright, the right leg returns to fifth position in front and the pose écartée derrière is concluded in the initial position. On 3 & 4 the initial position is held.

Pose écartée devant Initial position: fifth position, épaulement effacé, left leg in front.

On 1 &, the arms, opening on the upbeat, are raised through preparatory position to first position, the head inclines slightly towards the left shoulder. On 2 &, the right leg is stretched in the direction of point 2 of the class diagram, the right arm is raised in third position, the left one is opened in second position, the head, turning to the right, is raised slightly, the torso, increasing the 'pull up', keeping the hips level and the shoulders opened and lowered, is inclined slightly to the left, imparting to the pose a proud bearing. On 3 & 4 the pose écartée devant is held (both legs are held taut and turned out to the utmost). On 1 & of the second bar, the right arm is opened in second position, the torso is brought upright, the head remains turned to the right. On 2 &, both arms are lowered in preparatory position, the leg returns to fifth position behind and the pose is concluded in the initial position. On 3 & 4, the initial position is held.

Remarks The working leg is stretched in the pose and returns to fifth position according to the rules for battement tendu.

Together with the basic poses of the classical dance, one also studies the so-called 'small poses' which are utilised in a number of movements in the exercises of the classical dance. In such poses the character and rules of the basic poses are observed.

> *Example* In the small pose croisée devant, the arms, opening on the upbeat, are raised to first position on 1 &. On 2 &, the right arm is opened in second position, the head turns to the right, the left arm remains in first position, the right leg is stretched to the front. On 3 & 4 the pose croisée is held. On 1 & 2 of the second bar, the arms are lowered in preparatory position (the left one directly from first position), the right leg returns to fifth position. On 3 & 4 the initial position is held.

The small poses croisée derrière and effacée devant and derrière are executed according to the same rules, observing the character of each pose.

> *Example* In the small pose écartée derrière the arms, opening on the upbeat, are closed on 1 & in the raised preparatory position[1]. On 2 &, both arms are opened to the side, the head turns to the left, the right leg is stretched in the direction of point 4 of the class diagram, the torso, increasing the 'pull up', is inclined slightly to the left. On 3 & 4 the pose is held. On 1 & 2 of the second bar, both arms are lowered into the preparatory position, the torso is brought upright, the right leg returns to fifth position. On 3 & 4, the initial position is held.

The small pose écartée devant is executed according to the same rules, observing the character of the pose. When the arms are in second position, the palms of the hands are facing downwards.

Remarks The poses of the classical dance are studied from two to four times with each leg.

The character of the musical accompaniment is legato. With a time signature of 4/4, the movement is executed in two bars. With a time signature of 3/4, in four bars.

---

[1] When the raised preparatory position is required, the arms are opened to the side on the level of this position.

Temps lié

Temps lié cultivates the movement co-ordination and helps to develop the feeling for dance.

Temps lié en avant Initial position: fifth position, épaulement croisé, right leg in front.

On 1 &, the arms, opening on the upbeat, are closed in preparatory position simultaneously with demi plié in fifth position. On 2, the left leg remains in demi plié, the right one is stretched forward with a sliding movement in the direction of point 8 of the class diagram, the arms are raised in first position, the head inclines to the left, the eyes are directed towards the hands. On 3, the pointed toe, widening the distance between both feet, continues to slide forward and the weight is transferred smoothly onto the other leg, into the pose croisée derrière. On 4, the left leg is closed in fifth position, the arms and head maintain the croisée pose. On 1 & of the second bar, demi plié in fifth position with a turn en face, the right arm remains in second position, the left one is lowered in first position, the head inclines to the right, the eyes are directed towards the left hand. On 2, the left leg remains in demi plié, the right one is stretched to the side with a sliding movement, the left arm is opened in second position, the head turns to the left. On 3, the pointed toe, increasing the distance between both feet, continues to slide to the side and the right foot is placed smoothly on the floor, as the left leg is stretched, the toe touching the floor. The centre of the body weight is transferred to the right leg, the position of the arms and the turn of the head are held. On 4, the left leg is closed in fifth position in front, the arms are lowered into the preparatory position and temps lié is concluded in épaulement croisé with the left leg in front, from where the movement is continued with the other leg.

Temps lié en arrière Initial position: as described above.

On 1 &, the arms, opening on the upbeat, are closed in preparatory position simultaneously with demi plié in fifth position. On 2, the right leg remains in demi plié, the left one is stretched to the back, with a sliding movement, in the direction of point 4 of the class diagram; the arms are raised in first position, the head inclines slightly to the left and the eyes are directed towards the hands. On 3, the pointed toe, increasing the

59

distance between both feet, continues to slide backwards and the weight is transferred smoothly onto the other leg, into the pose croisée devant. On 4, the right leg is closed in fifth position, the arms and head maintain the pose croisée. On 1 of the second bar, demi plié in fifth position with a turn en face, the right arm remains in second position, the left one is lowered in first position, the head inclines slightly to the right, the eyes are directed towards the left hand. On 2, the right leg remains in demi plié, the left one is stretched to the side with a sliding movement, the left arm is opened in second position, the head turns to the left. On 3, the pointed toe, increasing the distance between both feet, continues to slide sideways and the left foot is placed smoothly on the floor; as the right one is stretched with the toe touching the floor, the centre of the body weight is transferred to the left leg, the position of the arms and the turn of the head are held. On 4, the right leg is closed in fifth position behind, the arms are lowered into the preparatory position and temps lié is concluded in épaulement croisé, with the left leg in front; from here the movement is continued with the other leg.

Remarks Temps lié is studied immediately in the centre of the room (au milieu). From the denomination 'temps lié', it should be clear that a complete flow of movement is necessary. Having obtained expressiveness of the body in the poses and positions, the torso should remain 'pulled up', the shoulders opened and lowered, the legs turned out and the positions of the arms correct.

The rhythmical design, coinciding with the demands of temps lié, should be smooth, legato. With a time signature of 4/4, temps lié is executed in two bars. Afterwards a 3/4 time may be used, executing temps lié in eight bars.

Pas de bourrée

Pas de bourrée is the basic movement of an old French folk dance, its style changed according to the rules of the balletic idiom. Pas de bourrée develops the mobility and liveliness of the feet and it also gives a sharpness and adroitness to the movements of the legs. The study of pas de bourrée is started facing the barre. Having acquired clarity of execution, it is transferred to the centre of the room. At first the movement is concluded opening the arms in the direction of second position; afterwards in the small poses.

Pas de bourrée en dehors Initial position: fifth position, épaulement croisé, right leg in front.

Préparation on two introductory chords. On 1, the arms, opening on the upbeat, are closed in the raised preparatory position; the head inclines to the left, the eyes are directed towards the hands. On 2, the right leg executes demi plié, the left one is raised sur le cou-de-pied derrière; the arms, preserving their curve, are opened in the direction of second position, the head turns to the right. On 1, turn en face, the left leg steps onto a high demi-point, replacing the right one which is raised to the conditional cou-de-pied position; the arms are raised through the preparatory position into first position. On 2, the right leg transfers to a high demi-point, approximately halfway into second position, the left leg is raised to the conditional cou-de-pied position; the position of arms and head is not changed. On 3, the torso is turned in épaulement croisé, the left leg is lowered in demi plié, replacing the right one which is raised sur le cou-de-pied derrière; the right arm, preserving the curve, is opened in the direction of second position, the left one remains in first position, the head turns to the left. On 4, the position is held and pas de bourrée is then continued with the other leg (fig. 30).

Pas de bourrée en dedans Initial position: as described above.

Préparation on two introductory chords. On 1, the arms, opening on the upbeat, are closed in the raised preparatory

fig. 30   Pas de bourrée en dehors

position; the head inclines to the left, the eyes are directed towards the hands. On 2, the left leg executes demi plié, the right one is raised to the conditional cou-de-pied position; the arms, maintaining the curve, are opened in the direction of second position; the head turns to the right.

On 1, turn en face, the right leg steps onto a high demi-point, replacing the left leg which is raised sur le cou-de-pied derrière; the arms are raised through the preparatory position into first position.

On 2, the left leg transfers to a high demi-point, about half way into second position, the right leg is raised sur le cou-de-pied derrière; the position of arms and head is not changed. On 3, the torso is turned in épaulement croisé; the right leg is lowered in demi plié, replacing the left one which is raised to the conditional cou-de-pied position; the left arm, maintaining the curve, is opened in the direction of second position, the right one remains in first position, the head turns to the left. On 4, the position is held and pas de bourrée is then continued with the other leg.

Remarks In pas de bourrée the torso is 'pulled up', the legs, on demi-point, are taut and turned out, the instep and toes sur le cou-de-pied are fully stretched and the entire leg is turned out to the utmost.

The character of the musical accompaniment is very sharp (staccato). At first the time signature is 4/4, later on 3/4.

Arabesques

Arabesque is a patterned ornament in imitation Arab style. As a term in classical dance, arabesque is applied to certain poses which are described below. Four arabesques exist in classical dance, of which three are studied in the first year when organising the correct placement of arms and legs. The working leg in this case is not raised off the floor, which is why the arabesque does not have the expressiveness that belongs to it, introducing only a sketch of the pose.

First arabesque Initial position: fifth position, left leg in front, the body is directed towards point 7 of the class diagram, the arms are in the preparatory position, the head is turned to the right.

On 1 & 2, the arms, opening on the upbeat, are raised through preparatory position into first position, the head inclines slightly to the left, the eyes are directed towards the hands. On 3, the right arm is opened in second position and the right leg is stretched backwards towards point 3 of the class diagram. On 4, the hands are turned with the palms facing down, the line of the arms is softened a little at the elbows; the head is straight, the eyes are directed forward, continuing the line of the left arm. On 1 & 2 of the second bar, first arabesque is held. On 3 & 4, the arms are gradually lowered into the preparatory position, the right leg returns to fifth position and arabesque is concluded in the initial position.

Second arabesque Initial position: as described above.

On 1 & 2, the arms, opening on the upbeat, are raised through the preparatory position into first position, the head inclines slightly to the left, the eyes are directed towards the hands. On 3 & 4, the right leg is stretched backwards towards point 3 of the class diagram; the left arm is opened in second position, as the torso increases its 'pull up', the left shoulder is drawn slightly backwards, the hands are turned with the palms facing down, the line of the arms is softened a little at the elbows; the head turns to the right, the eye direction coincides with the turn of the head. On 1 & 2 of the second bar the arabesque is held. On 3 & 4, the arms are lowered into preparatory position, the right leg returns into fifth position and arabesque is concluded in the initial position.

Third arabesque Initial position: fifth position, épaulement croisé, right leg in front.

On 1 & 2, the arms, opening on the upbeat, are raised through the preparatory position, into first position, the head inclines slightly to the left and the eyes are directed towards the hands. On 3, the right arm is opened in second position, the left leg is stretched croisé derrière. On 4, the hands are turned with the palms facing down, the line of the arms is softened a little at the elbows, the head turns straight, the eyes are directed forward, continuing the line of the left arm. On 1 & 2 of the second bar, arabesque is held . On 3 & 4, the arms are lowered into preparatory position, the left leg returns to fifth position and arabesque is concluded in the initial position. All three arabesques are studied with the right leg as well as with the left one. The working leg is stretched in arabesque and returns into fifth position according to the rules for battement tendu.

Remarks In arabesque the torso is 'pulled up', the shoulders, remaining level, are opened and lowered. The arms are located on one level: the arm which is directed forward is kept on a straight line, the arm which is opened to the side continues the line of the shoulder. The hands, turned with the palms facing down, continue the line of the arms, the elbows are softened.

Allegro (jumps)

Jumps are the most difficult part of the classical dance class. In the first year, jumps are studied after one has acquired strength, resilience and turnout of the legs in demi plié, as well as a correctly placed torso.

Temps levé
Temps levé is a jump on the spot. Initial position: first position, en face, the torso is 'pulled up', the knees are fully stretched, the arms are in the preparatory position, the head is straight.

On 1 & 2, the legs, increasing the turnout, reach the maximum bend of the ankle joint in demi plié, the heels are pressed firmly into the floor, the torso is straight and 'pulled up'.[1] On &, the legs forcefully push away from the floor; in the jump the knees, instep and toes are stretched immediately and, resisting the pull of gravity, are fixed in first position in the air.

fig. 31   Temps levé sauté

On 3 &, the jump is concluded in demi plié; the legs transfer through the toes onto the whole foot.

---

[1] In all jumps in classical dance, demi plié, before the jump as well as after, is executed strictly according to the rules stated.

On 4, the knees, sustaining the turnout, are stretched slowly, and the legs return to the initial position (fig. 31).

Temps levé is studied in first, second and fifth positions.

Remarks In demi plié before the jump, the heels must be pressed into the floor particularly forcefully, with a complete turnout of the legs. This eliminates the absolutely unacceptable so-called 'double plié' and imparts strength to the legs in the jump. In the air the legs must be stretched to the utmost, fixing the position. At the moment of leaving the floor the torso is 'pulled up' and at ease. The arms are held freely and they maintain a correct preparatory position without any tension.

A thorough application of the rules in temps levé in all positions *is the foundation for all jumps in classical dance.*

At first, temps levé is studied facing the barre in first position. Yet, in executing the jump, one should preserve its independence, not leaning heavily on the barre with the hands. After mastering the tautness of the legs in the air and the resilience of the demi plié after the jump, the exercise is transferred to the centre of the room.

The time signature is 4/4. In the music two elements are combined: the demi plié is accompanied smoothly, the jump is accentuated energetically and briskly. At first, temps levé is executed in one bar. Afterwards, two jumps are done to one bar: on 1, demi plié, on &, a jump; on 2, demi plié, on &, a jump; on 3 &, demi plié; on 4, stretch in the initial position.

Changement de pieds

Having mastered temps levé in the positions one should proceed to the study of changement de pieds, which is a jump from fifth position changing the legs in the air.

Initial position: fifth position, right leg in front; the arms are in the preparatory position, the head is turned to the right.

On 1, demi plié. On &, the legs forcefully push away from the floor, and in the jump the knees, instep and toes are immediately stretched. The head turns en face. The taut legs, resisting the pull of gravity, and increasing turnout, are changed, opening only far enough not to touch one another. On 2 &, changement de pieds is concluded in fifth position in demi plié, the left leg in front with the head turned to the left. On 3 &, the legs are stretched, returning to the initial position. On 4, the initial position is held and changement de pied is then repeated with the left leg.

At first, changement de pieds is studied facing the barre. Having mastered the changing of the legs in the air and the resilience of the demi plié after the jump, the movement is transferred to the centre of the room. In demi plié before changement de pieds the heels are pressed firmly into the floor; in the jump the torso and the arms are held easily.

The time signature is 4/4. Changement de pieds is executed like temps levé: at first one jump to one bar, afterwards two jumps to one bar.

Pas échappé in second position

Pas échappé is a jump with an escaping movement. It is studied in second position when temps levé in second and fifth positions have been mastered.

Initial position: fifth position, right leg in front; the arms are in the preparatory position, the head is turned to the right.

On 1, demi plié, the head turns en face. On &, the legs push forcefully away from the floor, in a high jump in fifth position which is fixed in the air. On 2, the legs, stretched to the utmost, resisting the pull of gravity and increasing the turnout, are opened, landing in second position demi plié. On &, the legs, without releasing the muscles, forcefully push away from the floor in a high jump, fixing second position in the air. On 3, the fully taut legs, resisting the pull of gravity and increasing the turnout, are brought together, concluding the jump in fifth position demi plié, the left leg in front, with the head turned to the left. On 4, the legs are straightened and échappé is then repeated with the left leg (fig. 32).

Remarks The demi plié in fifth, and especially in second position, must be resilient and uninterrupted; the heels must be pressed firmly into the floor while the legs are turned out to the utmost. This excludes the possibility of a 'double demi plié' before the jump and retains the strength of the legs for the jump. The torso is 'pulled up' and at ease. especially during the jump from second position into fifth. The arms sustain the preparatory position without any tension.

fig. 32   Pas echappé

At first, échappé is studied facing the barre. After mastering the correctness and clarity of the transition from position to position during the jump, the movement is transferred to the centre of the room.

The time signature is 4/4. In the music, the same as for the previous jumps, two qualities are combined: smooth and brisk. Echappé is executed in one bar. Later on it is possible to execute échappé still to one bar of 4/4 time, but beginning the demi plié on the upbeat. Upbeat 2/8. On the first 1/8, demi plié; on the second 1/8, a jump in fifth position. On 1, demi plié in second position. On &, a jump in second position. On 2, demi plié in fifth position. On 3 &, the knees are straightened. 4 & is the upbeat for the next échappé.

Pas assemblé

Pas assemblé – an assembled jump – is more complicated than the previous jump. That is why one proceeds to its study only when one has mastered the stretched positions of the legs in the air.

Initial position: fifth position, right leg behind; the arms are in the preparatory position, the head is turned to the left. On 1, demi plié in fifth position, the head turns en face. On &, the right leg, sliding with the entire foot along the floor, is thrown to the side; at the same time the left leg pushes away from the floor, forcefully stretching the knees, instep and toes in the jump. On 2

fig. 33   Pas assemblé

&, both legs, resisting the pull of gravity and increasing the turnout, are brought together in fifth position in the air with the right leg in front. The assemblé is concluded in fifth position demi plié, the head is turned to the right. On 3 &, the knees are straightened slowly and the legs return to the initial position. On 4, the position is held, after which assemblé is executed with the other leg (fig. 33).

Pas assemblé in the opposite direction is executed from fifth position, beginning the movement with the leg which is in front and concluding it in fifth position behind.

Remarks Both legs are fixed in fifth position in the air at the moment of the jump, as assemblé is a jump from two legs onto two. The leg sliding to the side should be directed exactly in a straight line. The jump is concluded on the spot, without travelling forward or backwards. During the execution of assemblé the heels, before the jump as well as after it, are pressed firmly into the floor. The torso is 'pulled up' and at ease. The arms are held in the preparatory position, avoiding tension, particularly at the moment of the jump.

The study of pas assemblé is commenced facing the barre, transferring it shortly afterwards to the centre of the room. Too prolonged a study of assemblé at the barre deprives it of its independence.

The character of the musical accompaniment is similar to that of the previous jumps. The time signature is 4/4. Assemblé is executed in one bar. Once it has been mastered, in one bar of 2/4. On 1, demi plié; on &, the jump; on 2, demi plié; on &, straighten etc.

Pas balancé

Pas balancé is a rocking movement; it develops freedom and ease of co-ordination of the entire body.

Initial position: fifth position, right leg in front, arms in the preparatory position, the head turned to the right.

On the upbeat, on 3, demi plié in fifth position. On &, the left leg, sliding with the foot along the floor, is opened to the side. At the same time the right leg is straightened, the arms, rising slightly, are opened in second position, the head turning to the left. On 1, the left leg, lengthening the movement to the side, transfers to demi plié; the right leg is raised sur le cou-de-pied derrière. The torso (keeping the shoulders and hips level) inclines to the left; the right arm is closed in first position, the head remains turned to the left. On 2, the right leg, replacing the left one, transfers to demi-point, the left one is raised slightly from the floor; the position of arms, torso and head is held. On 3, demi plié on the left leg. On &, the right leg is opened to the side via the cou-de-pied derrière, sliding along the floor, the left leg is straightened; the right arm is opened in second position, the head turns to the right and pas balancé is executed to the other side.

After mastering the basic rules for pas balancé, it is executed with the arms in third position.

On the upbeat, the left leg is opened to the side, the arms are opened in second position. On 1, demi plié on the left leg, the right arm is closed in third position, the left one remains in second, the head remains turned to the left. On 3, at the same time as the right leg stretches to the side, the right arm is opened in second position. On 1, demi plié on the right leg; the left arm is closed from second position into third, the right arm remains in second position, the head remains turned to the right etc.

Remarks Pas balancé demands a smooth execution, turned out legs, correct arm positions and exact positions of the head

Pas balancé is studied in the centre of the room immediately, but at first the girls can hold their skirts between thumb and forefinger, preserving curved arm positions; the boys put their hands on their waist.

The musical beat is 3/4. A slow waltz. Pas balancé is executed in one bar.

Sissonne simple

Sissonne simple is a simple jump from two legs onto one.

Initial position: fifth position, right leg in front; the arms are in the preparatory position, the head is turned to the right.

On 1, demi plié; on &, a high jump according to the rules for temps levé, the head turning to the front: the fully stretched legs are fixed in fifth position in the air. On 2 &, resisting the pull of gravity, demi plié on the left leg, the right one assumes the conditional cou-de-pied position. On 3 &, the left leg is straightened, the right one is opened to the side with the toe on the floor and on 4 it is closed in fifth position behind, according to the rules for battement tendu; the head turns to the left.

fig. 34   Sissonne simple

Afterwards sissonne simple is executed with the left leg (fig. 34). Sissonne simple is also executed ending sur le cou-de-pied derrière at the conclusion of the jump.

At first, sissonne simple is studied facing the barre, transferring it to the centre of the room as soon as the pupils have mastered the resilience of the demi plié and the turnout of both legs at the conclusion of the jump (principle of battement fondu). The torso and arms are easy, as in other jumps. Later on, sissonne simple is executed followed by pas assemblé: at first facing the barre, afterwards in the centre of the room. After sissonne simple, the leg which is sur le cou-de-pied is lowered in fifth position demi plié and sliding the foot it is sent to the side in pas assemblé dessous.

After sissonne simple in the opposite direction it is followed by pas assemblé dessus.

The time signature is 4/4. The accompaniment underlines the fluidity of the demi plié and the briskness of the jump. Sissonne simple is executed in one bar. Sissonne simple with pas assemblé is also executed in one bar. On 1, demi plié; on &, the jump; on 2, demi plié; on & 3, assemblé; on & 4, the straightening of the legs.

Pas jeté

Initial position: fifth position, the right leg behind, the arms in the preparatory position, the head turned to the left.

On 1, demi plié in fifth position, the head turns en face. On &, the right leg, sliding with the foot along the floor, is thrown to the side, simultaneously the left leg pushes away from the floor; during this the knees, insteps and toes are forcefully stretched; in the air, the tautness and turnout of both legs are fixed. On 2 &, the right leg alights in demi plié replacing the left leg, which is bent sur le cou-de-pied derrière; the head is turned to the right. On 3 &, the right leg is straightened, the left one being joined to it is lowered into fifth position behind. On 4, the position is held, after which pas jeté in the opposite direction is begun with the leg which is in front, bending the other one in the conditional cou-de-pied position.

Remarks In pas jeté the leg slides to the side exactly in a straight line (principle of battement tendu jeté). The jump is executed without travelling forwards or backwards. In demi plié, before as well as after the jump, the feet are firmly pressed into the floor. In the jump, particularly at the moment of its conclusion, the legs are turned out, the torso is pulled up and easy, the arms are held in an easy preparatory position.

At first pas jeté is studied facing the barre, transferring it to the centre of the room as soon as the pupils have mastered the resilience of the demi plié and the turnout of the legs at the conclusion of the jump.

The time signature is 4/4. Pas jeté is executed in one bar. The accompaniment underlines the fluidity of demi plié and the briskness of the jump.

Exercices sur les pointes

The technique of dancing on point plays an important role in the female dance. This is why exercises on point should be started from the first year of study, but not before the pupil has mastered the correct placement of the torso, arms and head, tautness and turnout of the legs and, most importantly, has sufficiently strong feet, with well-developed insteps. One should start with the simplest of exercises, which include relevés in first, second and fifth positions. At first, relevé on point is studied at the barre, without leaning on it with the hands. After mastering the correct position of the foot on point, the exercises are transferred to the centre of the room.

Relevé sur les pointes in first position

Initial position: first position, arms in the preparatory position.

On 1 & 2, demi plié in first position; the turnout of the legs is increased, the heels are pressed firmly into the floor, the torso is 'pulled up', maintaining the vertical line of the spine. On 3 &, the legs and feet push away from the floor onto point, immediately stretching the knees and insteps. On 4 &, first position on point is held. On 1 & 2 of the second bar, the legs, increasing the turnout, are lowered into first position in demi plié. On 3 & 4, they are straightened, returning to the initial position.

Remarks The distance between the heels in first position on point must be such that one can, when lowering the heels, return into first position without changing the position of the legs. Relevé in second and in fifth positions is executed according to the same rules. Here also the maximum turnout and tautness of the legs is demanded. The insteps are well arched and the positions of the legs on point must be correctly established. In relevé in fifth position, the legs are joined together so firmly that the optical impression of one leg is suggested.

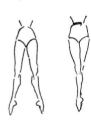

fig. 35 Relevé

In relevé, especially in second position, it is necessary to ensure the equal distribution of the body weight over two legs. In order to avoid 'sickling' the instep inward, one must stand on the first and second toes, maintaining the turnout of the heels. The utmost tautness and turnout of the legs on point, together with a 'pulled up' and easily held torso, help to develop stability (fig. 35). The demi plié, as in jumps, is resilient and continuous; the heels are pressed firmly into the floor with completely turned out legs; this makes the legs strong, facilitating the relevé on point. The torso and arms are totally at ease.

The transition from one position to another is executed at first by means of battement tendu, on two chords; later, by means of relevé on point in second position at the end of the musical phrase.

The character of the musical accompaniment is brisk, energetic. The time signature is 4/4. At first relevé is executed in two bars, later in one bar: on 1, demi plié; on & 2, relevé; on & 3, demi plié; on 4, straighten.

Pas échappé sur les pointes

Initial position: fifth position, right leg in front, arms in the preparatory position, head turned to the right.

On 1 & 2 &, demi plié in fifth position. On 3 &, the legs, pushing away from the floor, rise on point in second position, opening evenly and simultaneously; during this the knees, insteps and toes are forcefully stretched and the head turns to the left. On 4 &, second position on point is held. On 1 & 2 & of the second bar, the legs are closed simultaneously into fifth position in demi plié, left leg in front, with the head turned to the left. On 3 & 4, the legs are straightened and the movement is concluded. Echappé is now executed with the left leg. Echappé in second position is studied both with and without a change of the legs. In échappé without changing the legs, the initially assumed turn of the head is maintained. In échappé changing the legs, the turn of the head is changed with the relevé on point in second position.

Remarks

When executing échappé the legs, both in demi plié and on point, maintain their turnout, the torso is 'pulled up', thus facilitating the relevé on point. The torso and arms are totally at ease, the head is turned freely.

The character of the musical accompaniment is very brisk and energetic. The time signature is 4/4. At first, one échappé is executed in two bars, later in one

Pas de bourrée sur les pointes changing the legs en dehors and en dedans

Pas de bourrée changé on point is studied in the same way as pas de bourrée changé on demi-point; at first facing the barre, later in the centre of the room. The time signature and the character of the musical accompaniment are similar to the accompaniment of pas de bourée on demi-point.

Pas suivi

Pas suivi is an uninterrupted run on point in fifth position. In the first year a simplified form of pas suivi is studied sur place (on one spot); at first at the barre, later, when the movement is clearly established, in the centre of the room.

Initial position: fifth position épaulement croisé, right leg in front; the torso is 'pulled up', the hands hold the skirt between forefinger and thumb, the head is turned to the right.

Two introductory chords. On the first chord, demi plié in fifth position. On the second, relevé in fifth position. On the upbeat, on &, the left leg, barely bending the knee, is slightly raised off the floor; on 1, it returns to the same spot, immediately stretching the knee. Both legs repeat the movement as clearly as possible, maintaining a turned out fifth position in épaulement croisé. At the end of the musical phrase the pupil comes off point into fifth position. At first pas suivi is executed slowly, gradually increasing in speed as the pupil masters the movement.

The character of the musical accompaniment is clear, lively. The time signature is 2/4: at first each movement takes 1/8, afterwards 1/16 of a bar.

Pas suivi en tournant

Initial position: fifth position, épaulement croisé, right leg in front.

On two introductory chords relevé on point in fifth position, the skirt is held between forefinger and thumb. Maintaining the turnout in fifth position on point and the 'pull up' of the torso, one should turn to the right according to the rules for pas de bourrée suivi, revolving 360° around one's own axis, remaining sur place. At the beginning of each turn, the head turns to the left and, without delay, returns to the right. On two concluding chords, return to the initial position.

Remarks The turn should not be executed faster than in one bar of 4/4. Each 1/4 of the bar must coincide with 1/4 of the turn, which ensures the evenness of the turn of the legs, torso and head.

The time signature is 4/4 or 3/4. The character of the music is light, clear and lively.

Pas couru

Pas couru is a run on point, but, differing from pas suivi, it is executed in a parallel position. Apart from this, pas couru is executed only forwards and backwards, distinguishing it from pas suivi which is also executed sideways. Pas couru is studied at the barre, and is only transferred to the centre of the room when the clarity of the movement has been established.

Initial position: fifth position, épaulement croisé, right leg in front, the torso is 'pulled up', forefinger and thumb holding the skirt, the head is turned to the right.

Two introductory chords. On the first chord, demi plié; on the second, relevé in the parallel position (fig. 36). On the upbeat, on &, the right leg, barely bending the knee, is slightly raised from the floor; on 1, it returns to the same spot, immediately stretching the knee. On &, the left leg, barely bending the knee, is slightly raised from the floor; on 2, it returns to the same spot, immediately stretching the knee. Both legs repeat the movement as accurately as possible until the end of the musical phrase, slowly at first, later gradually increasing in speed as the pupil masters the movement. The exercise is concluded after the end of the musical phrase in fifth position in demi plié.

fig. 36
The leg
position for
pas couru

When clarity and purity in pas couru on the spot have been achieved, it is executed travelling forwards and backwards. Here also the shift from one foot to the other should be as tiny as possible, the torso remaining, 'pulled up' and easy. In pas couru moving straight forward, the arms are gradually raised from the preparatory to first position, the head inclines slightly to the left, the eyes are directed towards the hands; later, the arms are either opened in second position or raised in third. The head is slightly raised, the glance is directed to the front. In pas couru moving straight back, the arms are opened in second position and drawn slightly backwards; the torso is inclined slightly forward.

In pas couru forward on a diagonal from point 4 to point 8 of the class diagram, the arms are smoothly raised from the preparatory position into the first on 1 & 2; the head inclines to the left, the eyes are directed towards the hands. On 3 & 4, the run on points is continued, the right arm is smoothly raised in third position, the left one is opened in second position; the head, turning to the right, is inclined slightly forward, the eyes are directed under the right arm, past the elbow. On 1 & 2 of the second bar the run is continued in the same pose. On 3 & 4, concluding the movement, the right arm is gradually opened in second position, the head turning to the right in profile. On 1 & 2 of the following bar, pas couru is commenced on the same diagonal, travelling backwards; the hands, opening, are turned with the palms facing down and the arms are drawn back slightly; the 'pulled up' torso is inclined slightly forward. The pose is sustained until the end of the musical phrase. Pas couru from point 6 to point 2 of the class diagram is executed according to the same rules.

The character of the musical accompaniment is light, lively and brisk. The time signature is 4/4, 2/4 or 3/4; the movement is counted in sixteenths.

The Second Year of Study

The exercises of the second class

The basic aims of the second year are: the development of strength in the feet by means of exercises on demi-point and on point; the development of stability; the development of strength in the legs by increasing the number of movements covered; the development of technique by executing the movements in a faster tempo.

In order to develop co-ordination, a number of exercises are gradually taken in épaulement, in the centre of the room.

Exercises en face and in épaulement are combined, both at the barre and in the centre (not more than two at first).

As well as developing co-ordination, the combination of movements cultivates the feeling of dance. This is why the combination of the movements should be varied, as the daily repetition of the same combinations produces a mechanical manner of execution. But it is also necessary to repeat the movement in its original form, in order to check the correctness of execution. The movements which appear for the first time in the second year syllabus are at first studied in their basic form.

The musical accompaniment of the lessons in the second year demands, as compared to those in the first year, more variation of rhythmical design and a general acceleration of tempo. When movements are combined, the general melodic line is maintained, varying only the rhythmical design within the bar, thus illustrating the character of the amalgamated movements.

Exercices à la barre

The exercises at the barre in the second year are a repetition and a development of those of the first year. Having acquired stability on the whole foot, the individual movements are now transferred to demi-point, achieving stability in that position, and strengthening the legs.

Having mastered the correct placement of the foot[1] on demi-point, it is raised to its maximum height. A high demi-point ensures the tautness of the supporting leg and the 'pull up' of the torso, imparting lightness and harmony to the figure of the dancer. A preparatory exercise, relevé on demi-point on one leg, is executed at the conclusion of the exercises at the barre, facing it.

Example Initial position: fifth position, right leg in front; the torso is 'pulled up', the hands are resting lightly on the barre.

fig. 37
The position
of the leg
on demi-point

On two introductory chords, the right leg is stretched to the side with the toe on the floor, and is then bent sur le cou-de-pied devant or derrière. On 1 & 2, the heel of the taut supporting leg, maintaining the turnout, is raised gradually from the floor as high as possible, thus arching the instep. While on demi-point, avoid putting the weight on the big toe; the working leg maintains an accurate cou-de-pied position. On 3 & 4, the position is held. On 1 & 2 of the second bar, the supporting leg is gradually lowered onto the floor. On 3 & 4, the position is held (fig. 37).

Relevés on demi-point are repeated from four to eight times. Afterwards, slow relevés on demi-point are combined with fast ones, alternating relevés taking two quarters and relevés taking one quarter of a bar each.

Remarks In relevé it is necessary to watch the correct placement of the foot on the floor, avoiding putting the weight on the big toe, and also ensuring the utmost degree of tautness and turnout in the supporting leg. The 'pull up' of the torso and the forcefully stretched supporting leg allow the heel to be raised easily from the floor, maintaining its turnout. The hands are resting lightly on the barre; the pupils should not lean on it.

Having mastered relevé on demi-point on one leg, facing the barre, it is now executed holding on to the barre with one hand. It is then introduced into the exercises: for example, petit

---

[1] See relevé on demi-point in the first year.

battement sur le cou-de-pied can now be performed on demi-point.

After mastering relevé on demi-point sur le cou-de-pied devant and derrière, the movement is executed with the working leg at an angle at 45°, in all directions, thus preparing for more complicated exercises on demi-point. This form of relevé is combined with battement frappé and battement fondu.

Petit battement on demi-point

The execution of petit battement is preceded by a préparation. Initial position: fifth position, right leg in front. On 1, the arm, opening on the upbeat, is raised through the preparatory position into first. On &, the working leg is opened to the side, with the toe on the floor, the arm is opened in second position. On 2, the working leg is bent sur le cou-de-pied devant, the supporting leg rises to demi-point, the arm remains in second position. In petit battement the supporting leg is turned out (especially at the heel); the knee is stretched. The principles of the movement are the same as when it is executed on the whole foot.

Battement fondu on demi-point

In battement fondu, the relevé of the supporting leg coincides with the unfolding of the working leg – at 45°; the movement of both legs is completed simultaneously. In relevé the heel of the supporting leg is turned out, the placement of the foot on the floor is even, with no additional weight resting on the big toe. The heel of the supporting leg is raised from the floor only after the knee is stretched; the demi plié begins only after the heel touches the floor.

At first one should alternate battement fondu on the whole foot with battement fondu on demi-point. Afterwards battement fondu is executed exclusively on demi-point. The rules of execution are the same as when it is executed on the whole foot.

Battement frappé on demi-point

At the beginning of the study, battements frappés on the whole foot and on demi-point are alternated.

> *Example* On three quarters of the first bar, three battements frappés on the whole foot. On the fourth quarter, relevé on

demi-point with the working leg opened at 45° in the given direction. On three quarters of the second bar, three battements frappés on demi-point. On the fourth quarter, the heel is lowered to the floor, etc.

Afterwards battement frappé is executed on demi-point exclusively. In this case the préparation for battement frappé is also executed on demi-point.

On 1, the arm is raised in first position. On 2, the working leg, sliding with the entire foot along the floor, is opened to the side at 45°, the supporting leg is raised on demi-point, the arm is opened in second position.

At the end of the exercise, on two concluding chords, the working leg, sliding with pointed toes along the floor, is closed in fifth position behind, the heel of the supporting leg is lowered onto the floor, the arm is closed in the preparatory position.

Battement double frappé on demi-point

Battement double frappé is studied according to the rules for battement frappé. At the beginning of the movement, the relevé on demi-point coincides with the bending of the working leg sur le cou-de-pied. With the beat of the working foot, the demi-point is held. At the end of the movement the heel of the supporting leg is lowered onto the floor, the working leg is stretched out in the given direction, with the toe on the floor or at 45°. Afterwards the entire movement is executed on demi-point.

The musical accompaniment is the same as in the first year.

Rond de jambe en l'air on demi-point

At first rond de jambe en l'air on the entire foot and on demi-point are alternated. Afterwards the exercise is executed on demi-point exclusively. The préparation for rond de jambe en l'air is at first executed in two movements, stressing the transfer from the whole foot to the relevé.

Two introductory chords. On 1, the arm is raised in first position. On &, the working leg is stretched to the side, the arm is opened in second position. On 2, the working leg is raised at 45°, the supporting leg is raised on demi-point. The upbeat for the beginning of rond de jambe en l'air is on '&'. At the end of the exercise there are two concluding chords: on the first one the working leg is lowered with the toe on the floor as the supporting leg comes down with the heel on the floor; on the second chord, the working leg is closed into fifth position behind as the arm is lowered in preparatory position.

Later, both movements of the préparation are united. On 1, the arm is raised in first position; on 2, the working leg, sliding with the entire foot along the floor, is opened to the side at 45°, the supporting leg is raised on demi-point, the arm is opened in second position. The upbeat for the beginning of rond de jambe en l'air is on '&'. At the end of the exercise, on two concluding chords, the working leg, sliding the toe along the floor, is closed into fifth position behind, the supporting heel is lowered onto the floor, the arm is lowered in preparatory position.

Remarks In rond de jambe en l'air, the knee of the supporting leg is stretched and the heel in particular is turned out; the placement of the foot on demi-point is even, with no additional weight resting on the big toe.

The musical accompaniment is the same as that in the first year.

Battement soutenu at 45°

Initial position: fifth position.

Count 3/8 for the upbeat. On the first 1/8, the arm is opened slightly. On the second 1/8, it is closed in preparatory position, simultaneously rising on demi-point, in fifth position. On the third 1/8 the arm is raised in first position, the head inclining to the left; the working leg is raised to the conditional cou-de-pied position. On 1, the supporting leg, lowering the heel onto the floor, begins the demi plié; the working leg, maintaining the turnout, is stretched forward at 45°; the arm is opened in second position as the head turns to the right. On &, the supporting leg continues the demi plié, the working leg is lowered and touches the floor with pointed toes. On 2, without delay, it is pulled towards the supporting leg, returning to fifth position, at the same time as the supporting leg is straightened, both legs finishing simultaneously in fifth position on demi-point. The upbeat for the following battement soutenu is on the '&'.

Observing these rules, battement soutenu is executed in all directions. At the conclusion of the exercise, the arm is lowered in preparatory position together with the return of the legs into fifth position.

With battement soutenu, accompanying movements of arms and head can be introduced, not only at the beginning and at the conclusion of the exercise, but sometimes also in the middle. If battement soutenu is executed in one direction only, the arm remains in second position. With the transition to another direction, the arm is lowered from second into preparatory position simultaneously with the return of the legs into fifth position on demi-point; it is raised again in first position together with the bending of the leg sur le cou-de-pied. Battement soutenu at 45° to the front and to the back is executed with a turn of the head away from the supporting leg. With battement soutenu to the side, the head is en face.

When battement soutenu has been mastered at the barre, it is transferred in the same order to the centre of the room. At first, battement soutenu is executed exclusively en face; later in the poses croisée and effacée. The arms are opened through first position into the small poses,

Remarks It is essential that the supporting leg, coming down from demi-point, remains taut, beginning the demi plié only after the heel touches the floor. Also in fifth position on demi-point, the legs must be extremely taut and turned out. The 'pulled up' torso maintains the body weight centred over the supporting leg.

The time signature is 4/4. At first, one battement soutenu is executed in one bar, later on two.

Half turn in fifth position on demi-point (demi détourné)
Half turn in fifth position on demi-point trains the torso for all kinds of turns.

Half turn towards the barre Initial position: fifth position, right leg in front; the right arm is opened in second position, the head is turned to the right, the left arm is resting easily upon the barre.

On the upbeat, demi plié in fifth position. On 1, the 'pull up' of the torso is increased; the legs, in fifth position, are raised on high demi-point; the right arm is held in second position, the head turns en face, the eyes are directed straight ahead. On 2, the pupil makes a turn of 180° towards the barre. The legs in fifth position (maintaining their tautness and increasing the turnout of the heels) change in such a manner that by the end of the turn, the left leg is in front. At the beginning of the turn the arms are brought together in first position; at the conclusion the right hand is placed on the barre, the left arm is opened in second position. When the arms are united in first position, the head turns to the right; at the conclusion of the turn it is turned to the left. On 3, the position is fixed. On 4, demi plié, and then repeat the turn to the other side.

Half turn away from the barre Initial position: fifth position, right leg behind; the right arm is opened in second position, the head is turned to the right, the left hand is resting easily on the barre. On 1, the 'pull up' of the torso is increased; the legs, in fifth position, are raised on high demi-point, the head and arms remain in the position they have assumed. On 2, the pupil makes a turn of 180° away from the barre; the legs in fifth position, maintaining their tautness and increasing the turnout of the heels, change in such a manner that the left leg is behind at the conclusion of the turn. At the beginning of the turn the left arm is directed towards first position; at the conclusion of the movement it is opened in second position, the right hand is placed upon the barre, the head turns to the left. On 3, the position is held. On 4, demi plié, and then execute the turn to the other side.

Remarks The turn of the torso must coincide exactly with the turn of the legs. The exact co-ordination of the arms, head and eye direction stimulate the turn.

After the students have mastered the half turn, it is introduced in all the exercises at the barre, in the middle as well as at the conclusion of the combinations. The demi plié at the beginning of the half turn may take place on the count of 1 or on the upbeat.

Port de bras with rond de jambe soutenu
Having mastered rond de jambe soutenu, a port de bras is added to this exercise. At the conclusion of rond de jambe soutenu en dehors, on 4, the supporting leg is straightened, the working leg

remaining behind with the toe touching the floor opposite the heel of the supporting leg; the arms are held in second position, the head is turned to the left.

On 1 &, the supporting leg begins a gradual demi plié, as the stretched working leg slides with the toe to the back, exactly in a straight line. The turnout of both legs is held, and the 'pull up' of the torso is increased as it is directed forward; the arm is lowered; the head, which is turned to the left, is inclined with the eyes following the hand. On 2 &, the 'pulled up' torso, with the shoulders level, opened and lowered and continuing the movement, is inclined forward. The arm is closed in first position, the head turns en face and the eyes are directed towards the hand. On 3 & 4, the supporting leg returns from the deepened demi plié[1] into a normal demi plié; the taut working leg slides with the toe along the floor, the torso is brought gradually upright, the arm is raised in third position and the head turns to the right. On 1 & 2 of the second bar, the torso, keeping the shoulders opened and lowered, gradually bends back; the arm remains in third position and the head is turned to the right. On 3 & 4, the torso, having reached the deepest point of the backbend, is brought gradually upright, the arm is opened in second position and the supporting leg is straightened.

On a concluding chord, the working leg is closed in first or fifth position, the arms returning to the preparatory position. At the conclusion of rond de jambe soutenu en dedans, on 4, the supporting leg is straightened, the working leg remains stretched in front, the toe touching the floor opposite the heel of the supporting leg. The arm remains in second position and the head is turned to the right. On 1 &, the supporting leg begins a gradual demi plié, as the toe of the taut working leg slides forwards.

On 2 &, the 'pulled up' torso, with the shoulders level, opened and lowered, continuing the movement, bends forward. The arm is lowered into preparatory position, the head inclines, the eyes following the hand. On 3 & 4, the torso is brought gradually upright, the arm is raised through first position into third, the head turns to the right. On 1 & 2 of the second bar, the torso,

---

[1] The inclination forward of the torso in port de bras allows for a deepening of demi plié of the supporting leg without raising the heel off the floor.

keeping the shoulders opened and lowered, gradually bends back, the arm remaining in an exact third position. On 3 & 4, the torso, having reached the ultimate point of the backbend, is brought gradually upright, the arm opens in second position, the supporting leg is straightened. On a concluding chord, the working leg is closed in first or fifth position as the arm returns into preparatory position.

Remarks It is necessary to ensure that both legs are turned out at all times and that the torso is 'pulled up', keeping the weight of the body centred over the supporting leg while bending back.

Plié relevé at 45°
Plié relevé, as a rule, is combined with battement fondu, but sometimes also with other exercises of the classical dance. At the conclusion of the preceding movement the working leg is opened at 45° in any direction. The supporting leg (maintaining the turnout of both legs) executes demi plié and afterwards, without relaxing the muscles, is straightened and is raised on demi-point, the working leg maintaining the position it has assumed. Plié relevé may be repeated in the same direction, or the direction may be changed with the battement fondu. Having mastered plié relevé in all directions, one proceeds to plié relevé with demi rond de jambe, which is a more complicated form of this movement.

Plié relevé at 45° with demi rond de jambe
At the conclusion of the preceding movement (for example battement fondu) the working leg is opened in front at 45°. The supporting leg executes demi plié and, without relaxing the muscles, is raised on demi point. At the same time, the working leg, increasing the turnout, is brought to the side, sustaining the height of 45°. Plié relevé at 45° with demi rond de jambe is executed in all directions en dehors and en dedans.

Remarks In plié relevé, and in plié relevé with demi rond de jambe, the torso is 'pulled up' and the legs are turned out to the utmost, especially in rond de jambe en dehors. The hand rests easily upon the barre, and never changes its initial position.

The time signature and character of the music must correspond with the exercise with which the plié relevé is being combined.

Temps relevé at 45° en dehors and en dedans

Temps relevé at 45° is an auxiliary movement in the exercises of the classical dance. In the second year it is executed as préparation for rond de jambe en l'air.

Temps relevé at 45° en dehors Initial position: fifth position, right leg in front.

On 1, the arm is raised, through preparatory position into first position, executing a demi plié of the supporting leg and simultaneously raising the working leg to the conditional cou-de-pied position. The head inclines slightly to the left. On &, the working leg, increasing the turnout of the thigh and the heel, begins to move slightly forward. On 2, the working leg, continuing the movement and as if steering it, straightens and, without stopping, is brought to the side at 45°; as the supporting leg is straightened, the arm is opened in second position and the head is turned to the right. On &, the position is held.

Temps relevé at 45° en dedans Initial position: fifth position, right leg behind.

On 1, the right arm is raised through the preparatory position into first position, executing a demi plié of the supporting leg and simultaneously raising the working leg sur le cou-de-pied derrière. The head inclines slightly to the left. On &, the working leg, increasing the turnout of the thigh, immediately begins to move slightly back. On 2, the working leg, continuing the movement and as if steering it, straightens and without stopping is brought to the side at 45°; as the supporting leg is straightened, the arm opens in second position and the head is turned to the right.

Remarks In temps relevé the torso is 'pulled up', the supporting leg sustains a correct demi plié, particularly at the moment of bringing the leg to the side, and the working leg is extremely turned out in both directions.

If temps relevé is executed as préparation for rond de jambe en l'air, it is executed on two introductory chords. If temps relevé is combined with rond de jambe en l'air it is included in the musical phrase.

Having mastered this movement on the whole foot, it is executed on demi-point. The relevé on demi-point coincides with the moment of bringing the leg to the side.

The character of the musical accompaniment is energetic. The time signature is 2/4 or 4/4. When temps relevé is combined with rond de jambe en l'air, the energetic character of temps relevé is stressed by the music without disturbing the general melodic line.

Battement développé passé at 90°

Passé, which is a transition from one direction to another, or from one pose to another, is a connecting movement in exercises with the working leg at the height of 90°.

At the conclusion of battement développé or battement relevé lent, the working leg, which is extended at 90°, does not conclude the movement in fifth position but changes direction by means of passé. The working leg, increasing the turnout of the thigh, bends the knee, directing the pointed toe towards the level of the knee of the supporting leg. The toe of the working leg, maintaining the turnout of the heel, is drawn close to the supporting leg but does not touch it.

During the passé the torso increases its 'pull up', especially when the passé is executed from a position with the leg extended to the back at 90°. The working leg is moved into retiré in different ways, depending on the direction it was in before the passé, but the exact moment of passé is always the same: the toe located at the level of the knee of the supporting leg is always at the side, in order not to disturb the transition from one pose to another or from one direction to another. From the

fig. 38
Battement développé
passé at 90°

retiré position the working leg can repeat the movement in the preceding direction or change it according to the instructions (fig. 38).

It is imperative that the working leg, in spite of its bent position in retiré, remains firm. This ensures its independence and defines the quality of the following movement.

The time signature and character of the music are the same as those for battement développé or battement relevé lent.

Demi rond de jambe at 90°

One proceeds to this exercise having mastered battement relevé lent and battement développé in all directions.

Demi rond de jambe en dehors Initial position: fifth position, right leg in front.

On the upbeat, the right arm is opened. On 1 &, it is opened through preparatory position into first position, the head inclines slightly to the left, and the working leg is raised via the conditional cou-de-pied position to the middle of the knee of the supporting leg. On 2 &, the working leg is stretched to the front at 90°[1], the head and arm retaining their position. On 3 & 4 &, the working leg, gradually rising, is drawn to the side, the arm is opened in second position and the head turns to the right. On 1 & 2 & of the second bar, the position is held. On 3 &, the working leg is lowered into fifth position in front, the arm is closed into the preparatory position. On 4, the position is held. On &, the arm is opened. On 1 &, it is raised through the preparatory position into first position, the head inclines slightly to the left, the working leg is raised via the conditional cou-de-pied position to the middle of the knee of the supporting leg. On 2 &, the working leg is stretched to the side at 90°, the arm is opened in second position, the head turns to the right. On 3 & 4 &, the working leg, gradually rising, is drawn to the back. The 'pull up' of the torso increases as it is directed slightly forward. On 1 & 2 & of the second bar, the position is held. On 3 &, the working leg is lowered into fifth position behind, the torso is brought upright and the arm is closed into the preparatory position. On 4 &, the position is held.

Demi rond de jambe en dedans Initial position: fifth position, right leg behind.

On the upbeat the right arm is opened. On 1 &, it is raised through preparatory position into first position; the head inclines slightly to the left, the working leg is raised via the

---

[1] *See* battement développé in the first year.

cou-de-pied derrière to the back of the knee of the supporting leg.

On 2 &, the working leg is stretched to the back at 90°; during this, the torso resists the inevitable inclination and the head and arm maintain their position. On 3 & 4 &, the working leg, gradually rising, is drawn to the side, the 'pull up' of the torso is increased, the arm is opened in second position and the head turns to the right. On 1 & 2 & of the second bar, the position is held. On 3 &, the working leg is lowered into fifth position behind, the arm is closed into the preparatory position. On 4, the position is held. On &, the arm is opened. On 1 &, it is raised through the preparatory position into first position, the head inclines slightly to the left and the working leg is raised via the cou-de-pied derrière to the back of the knee of the supporting leg. On 2 &, the working leg is stretched to the side at 90°, the arm is opened in second position and the head turns to the right. On 3 & 4 &, the working leg, gradually rising, is drawn to the front. On 1 & 2 & of the second bar, the position is held. On 3 &, the working leg is lowered into fifth position in front, the arm is closed into the preparatory position. On 4 &, the position is held.

Remarks In demi rond de jambe at 90° the tautness and turnout of both legs are maintained; the centre of the body weight is placed exactly over the supporting leg, particularly when executing demi rond de jame en dedans from the back to second position. Both arms, the one resting on the barre and the one opened in second position, maintain their correct positions. Particular attention should be paid to the arms, as they tend to lose their correct form as the leg moves.

The time signature is 4/4. The character of the music is legato. At first, demi rond de jambe is executed in two bars. Once it has been mastered, in one bar of 4/4. On 1, the leg is raised to the knee; on 2, it is stretched in the given direction; on 3, it executes the demi rond de jambe; on 4, it is lowered.

Exercises in épaulement

Exercises in épaulement at the barre are studied first in the effacée poses, as their construction is the simplest. Later, one proceeds to the study of the croisée poses. At first, the exercises in épaulement start directly from épaulement. Therefore the pupil moves from the fifth position en face into épaulement on two introductory chords, before starting the exercise. Later, movements en face are alternated with movements in épaulement. All turns into épaulement demand an exact coordination of torso, legs, arms and head, in order to meet the requirements of the character of the pose; this should be sustained throughout the exercise. During the exercises in épaulement, it is important to ensure that the position of the supporting foot is correct.

Example Battement fondu in the small poses effacée devant and derrière, combined with battement frappé en face. The exercise is executed in sixteen bars. The time signature is 2/4.

First eight bars. On the first bar, battement fondu to the front. On the second bar, plié relevé with demi rond de jambe en dehors. On the third bar, battement fondu to the side. On the fourth bar, battement fondu effacé devant. On the turn into effacée, the supporting leg executes a demi plié, the working leg is bent in the conditional cou-de-pied position, the right arm is lowered in preparatory position; with the relevé on demi-point, it is raised in first position. At the beginning of the movement the head inclines, but at the end it is straightened: throughout, the eyes follow the hand which is opened a little at the end of the movement. On &, as the body turns en face, the working leg is bent sur le cou-de-pied; the arm is in first position, the head inclines to the left, the eyes are directed towards the hand. Now follow battements frappés: two to the front, two to the side, two to the back; the arm is opened in second position, the head turns en face. On the eighth bar, the exercise is concluded in fifth position behind; the right arm is lowered in preparatory position, the head turns to the right.

Second eight bars. On the first bar, battement fondu to the back. On the second bar, plié relevé with demi rond de jambe en dedans. On the third bar, battement fondu to the side. On the fourth bar, battement fondu effacée derrière. On the turn into effacée, the supporting leg executes a demi plié, the working leg is bent sur le cou-de-pied derrière, the right arm is lowered in preparatory position; with the relevé on demi-point it is raised in first position. At the beginning of the movement the head inclines, but at the end it turns to the right, the eyes following the hand. On &, as the body turns en face, the right leg is bent sur le cou-de-pied derrière, the arm is in first position; the head inclines to the left, the eyes are directed towards the hand. Now follow battements frappés: two to the back, two to the side, two to the front; the arm is opened in second position, the head turns en face. On the eighth bar, the exercise is concluded in fifth position in front. The arm is lowered in preparatory position, the head turns to the right.

Remarks The given example is not compulsory. Battements fondus can be done in any sequence, but the transition to the pose is the same; the beginning of battement fondu always coincides with the turn into épaulement. The correctness of the pose depends on the position of the supporting foot. This is why one should ensure that the heel of the supporting leg is slightly drawn back in the poses effacée devant and croisée derrière, and forcefully directed forward in the poses effacée derrière and croisée devant.

Small poses concluding the exercise

The small poses croisée, effacée and écartée are used to conclude several exercises at the barre and in the centre of the room They are executed either with a straight supporting leg or in demi plié, with the toe of the working leg pointed on the floor (fig. 39).

Example 1 Small pose effacée combined with petit battement. The exercise is executed in eight bars. The time signature is 4/4.

On two introductory chords, preparation. First four bars.

fig. 39   The small poses at the barre

On the first bar, four petits battements, accentuating on each 1/4 the cou-de-pied devant. On the first 1/4 of the second bar, petit battement; on the second, a pause sur le cou-de-pied devant. On the third 1/4, petit battement; on the fourth, a pause. On the first 2/4 of the third bar, two petits battements. On the third 1/4, a petit battement which is finished in the conditional cou-de-pied position. On the fourth 1/4, a turn to effacée: the right arm, being lowered, moves to the raised preparatory position, the head inclines to the left, the glance is directed at the right hand. On the first 1/4 of the fourth bar the supporting leg executes a demi plié; the working leg is stretched to the front in effacée with the toe on the floor, the 'pulled up' torso, with the shoulders opened, is inclined slightly forward. The right arm is opened in the direction of the toe of the working leg, the head is straightened, the eyes are directed towards the hand. On the second and third 1/4, the pose is held. On the fourth 1/4, with a turn en face, the supporting leg, having been straightened, executes a relevé on demi-point; the torso is brought upright, and the working leg is raised sur le cou-de-pied devant. The right arm is opened in second position, the head turns to the right.

Second four bars. The petits battements are continued, but now accentuating and pausing sur le cou-de-pied derrière. On the third 1/4 of the seventh bar, the petits battements are concluded sur le cou-de-pied derrière. On the fourth 1/4 there is a turn to effacée: the right arm is raised through the preparatory position into first, the head inclines towards the left shoulder, the eyes are directed towards the right hand. On the first 1/4 of the eighth bar the supporting leg executes a demi plié, the working leg is stretched in effacée derrière with the toe on the floor, the head turns to the right, keeping the weight of the body centred over the supporting leg; the torso bends gradually backwards at the waist, starting from the upper back. On the second and third 1/4 the pose is held. On the fourth 1/4, with a turn en face, the supporting leg, straightening, executes a relevé on demi-point; the working leg is raised sur le cou-de-pied derrière and the torso is brought upright. The arm is opened in second position, the head remains turned to the right. On two concluding chords, the supporting leg is lowered with the heel on the floor, the working leg is opened to the side with the toe on the floor and is closed in fifth position behind; the arm is lowered into the preparatory position.

Example 2 Small pose écartée, combined with rond de jambe en l'air en dehors and en dedans. The exercise is executed in eight bars. The time signature is 4/4.

First four bars. On 2/4 on the first bar, temps relevé en dehors; on the following five 1/4 ronds de jambe en l'air en dehors on 1/4 each. On the last 1/4 of the bar, a pause at 45°; the head turns to the right and inclines slightly, the eyes are directed towards the right hand. On 2/4 of the second bar, temps relevé is repeated. On the third 1/4, with a turn to effacée, the working leg is bent in the conditional cou-de-pied position. The right arm is lowered in the raised preparatory position, the head inclines to the left and the eyes are directed towards the right hand. On the fourth 1/4, the supporting leg executes a demi plié, the working leg is stretched in écartée derrière, with the toe on the floor. The right arm is opened in the direction of second position, the head turns to the left; the torso, increasing the 'pull up' and keeping the shoulders and hips level, inclines slightly to the left. On 2/4 of the fourth bar, the pose is held. On the third 1/4, the working leg is closed in fifth position behind, the right arm is lowered into the preparatory position. On the fourth 1/4, with a turn of the body en face, the head turns to the right.

Second four bars. On 2/4 of the fifth bar, temps relevé en dedans. On the following five 1/4, ronds de jambe en l'air en dedans on 1/4 each. On the last 1/4 of the sixth bar, a pause at 45°. The right arm is softened at the elbow, the hand is turned with the palm facing down, the head turns to the right and the eyes are directed towards the hand. On 2/4 of the following bar, temps relevé is repeated. On the third 1/4, with a turn to effacée, the working leg is bent sur le cou-de-pied derrière. The right arm is lowered in the raised preparatory position, the head inclines towards the left shoulder, the eyes are directed towards the right hand. On the fourth 1/4 the supporting leg executes a demi plié; the working leg is stretched in écartée devant, with the toe on the floor. The right arm, opening in the direction of second position, is softened at the elbow, the hand is turned with the palm facing down, the head turns to the right and the eyes are directed towards the hand. The torso, increasing the 'pull up' and keeping the shoulders and hips level, inclines slightly to the left. On 2/4 of the eighth bar, the pose is held. On the third 1/4, the working leg is closed in fifth position in front, the right arm is lowered into the preparatory position. On the fourth 1/4, with a turn of the body en face, the head turns to the right.

Remarks The examples given are not the only possible ones. The poses croisée, effacée and écartée can be interchanged, but the transition from the movement to the pose is always executed via the cou-de-pied. In the exercises and poses, it is compulsory that the legs are turned out, the torso is 'pulled up' and the shoulders and hips are level. The correctness of the pose depends on the position of the supporting foot. This is why it is necessary to ensure that the heel of the working leg is slightly drawn back in the poses effacée devant, croisée and écartée derrière, and forcefully directed forward in the poses effacée derrière, croisée and écartée devant.

In the centre of the room, the small poses conclude the exercise according to the same rules as at the barre. The transition from the exercise to the pose is executed via the cou-de-pied, the arms are opened via first position. In the pose écartée, the arms are opened at the level of the raised preparatory position. Poses on a straight supporting leg are executed according to the same rules.

Exercices au milieu

The exercises in the centre of the room are executed in the same order and with the same methodic approach as those at the barre. In order to master the exercises in épaulement, they are introduced in the centre practice. The croisée poses are studied first, as they are the simplest. The first exercises in épaulement, battement tendu and battement tendu jeté are executed in the croisée and effacée poses with the arms in the small and in the big poses. On two introductory chords the arms are opened in the pose, on two concluding chords they are lowered into the preparatory position. Later, the arms are opened in the pose and closed in the preparatory position during the course of the exercise.

>*Example* The anacrusis is divided into three 1/8. On the first 1/8 the arms are slightly opened; on the second 1/8 they are closed in the preparatory position. On the third 1/8, with the beginning of battement tendu, the arms are gradually opened through first position into the given pose. At the conclusion of the exercise, the arms are gradually lowered into the preparatory position.

Remarks When battement tendu is executed in the big poses, the arm from third position, concluding the movement, is gradually opened in second position and both arms are lowered into the preparatory position. When battement tendu is executed in the small poses, the arm is lowered from first position into the preparatory position simultaneously with the arm from second position. In battement tendu to the side, the arms are gradually opened through first position into second and then gradually lowered into the preparatory position, together with the last battement tendu.

The next exercises in épaulement are grand battement jeté and grand battement jeté piqué. These movements are executed with the arms in the big poses, opening them on two introductory chords, or on the anacrusis on three 1/8. On two concluding chords, the arms are lowered into the preparatory position, as indicated above.

After this follows battement fondu, in the small croisée and effacée poses where, as in the preceding exercises, the arms are at first opened in the pose beforehand and later, simultaneously with the battement fondu. If battement fondu is repeated several times in the same direction, the arms are held in position and are changed only with the transition to another direction or pose.

The rules of execution for demi rond de jambe en dehors and en dedans remain the same as those at the barre. Together with the développé to the front or to the back, both arms are raised in first position, opening with the beginning of demi rond de jambe into second position. When executing demi rond de jambe from second position en dehors or en dedans, the arms are opened in second position, together with the développé to the side.

Turn in fifth position, on demi-point, (détourné) in the centre of the room

Initial position: fifth position, épaulement croisé, right leg in front; the arms are opened in second position, the head is turned to the right.

On 1, demi plié in fifth position. On 2, the legs execute a relevé on high demi-point in fifth position; the arms remain in second position, the head remains turned to the right, the eyes are directed towards point 1 of the class diagram. On 3, a turn to the left towards point 2 of the class diagram, the legs in fifth position (sustaining the 'pull up' and increasing the turnout of the heels), are changed, so that at the end of the turn the left leg is located in front. At the beginning of the turn the arms are closed in first position, the eyes remaining directed at point 1 of the class diagram, but at the end of the turn the head is turned to the left as quickly as possible. On 4, the arms are opened in second position. On the following bar, the turn is executed to the other side.

Remarks It is compulsory that the turn of the torso coincides exactly with the turn of the legs. It is stimulated by an active turn of the head, the focus of the eyes and an exact co-ordination of the arms. The technique of pirouettes is ultimately dependent on the application of these rules.

Having mastered the turn, it is introduced into all the exercises of the classical dance, during as well as at the end of an exercise. The position of the arms at the conclusion of the turn depends on the instructions. The demi plié may be executed on the upbeat on &, and on the count of 1.

Poses of the classical dance at 90°

In the second year the poses of the classical dance are executed, raising the leg at an angle of 90°. In order to master them correctly and with more expression, they are studied immediately in the centre of the room, where their construction is more accurate than at the barre.

The poses of the classical dance are, as a rule, executed from the initial position épaulement croisé. Because of their complexity of construction, the poses effacée and écartée are initially studied starting from épaulement effacé. Having mastered the poses, they are then executed from épaulement croisé.

Pose croisée devant at 90° Initial position: fifth position, épaulement croisé, right leg in front, the arms are in the preparatory position, the head is turned to the right.

On 1 & 2 &, the arms, opening on the upbeat, are raised through the preparatory position into first position, the head inclines slightly to the left, the eyes are directed towards the hands. The working leg is raised via the conditional cou-de-pied position to the level of the knee. On 3 & 4 &, the working leg is extended forward in a continuous movement; the left arm is raised in third position, the right one is opened in second, the head turns to the right, the eyes follow the right hand. The torso, with the shoulders level, opened and lowered, is bent slightly backwards. On 1 & 2 & of the second bar, the pose is held. On 3 &, the left arm is opened in second position and both arms are lowered simultaneously with the leg. On 4 &, the movement is concluded in the initial position (fig. 40).

Pose croisée derrière at 90° Initial position: fifth position, épaulement croisé, left leg in front, the arms are in the preparatory position, the head is turned to the left.

On 1 & 2 &, the arms, opening on the upbeat, are raised through the preparatory position into first position, the head inclines slightly to the right, the eyes are directed towards the hands. The working leg (the right one) is raised via the cou-de-pied derrière to the level of the knee. On 3 & 4 &, the working leg, raised as high as possible, is stretched exactly in a straight line to the back; the right arm is raised in third position, the left one is opened in second, the head turns to the left. The torso, trying to resist the unavoidable inclination, increases the 'pull up'; the shoulders are level, opened and lowered. On 1 & 2 & of the second bar, the pose is held. On 3 &, the right arm is opened in second position and both arms are lowered simultaneously with the leg. On 4 &, the movement is concluded in the initial position.

The 'pull up' of the torso, the freely opened and lowered shoulders, the active turn of the head and the focused glance, impart an artistic look to the poses croisée devant and derrière.

Pose effacée devant at 90° Initial position: fifth position, épaule-

fig. 40   Croisée devant at 90°

ment croisé, right leg in front, the arms are in the preparatory position, the head is turned to the right.

On 1 & 2 &, the arms, opening on the upbeat, are raised, through the preparatory position, into first position simultaneously with a turn to effacée; the head inclines slightly to the left, the eyes are directed towards the hands; the working leg (the right one) is raised via the conditional cou-de-pied position to the level of the knee. On 3 & 4 &, the working leg is extended forward in a continuous movement; the left arm is raised in third position, the right one is opened in second, the head turns to the left. The torso, keeping the hips level and with the shoulders level, opened and lowered, is inclined slightly backwards. On 1 & 2 & of the second bar, the pose is held. On 3 &, the left arm is opened in second position, the torso is brought upright and both arms are lowered simultaneously with the leg. On 4 &, the movement is concluded in the initial position (fig. 41).

The slightly inclined torso, the freely lowered shoulders and the eye direction, which is in accordance with the turn of the head, impart an artistic look to the pose effacée devant.

Pose effacée derrière at 90°

Pose effacée derrière at 90° Initial position: fifth position, épaulement croisé, left leg in front, the arms are in the preparatory position, the head is turned to the left.

On 1 & 2 &, the arms, opening on the upbeat, are raised through the preparatory position into the first position, simultaneously with a turn to effacée; the head inclines slightly to the left, the eyes are directed towards the hands, the working leg (the right one) is raised via the cou-de-pied derrière to the knee. On 3 & 4 &, the working leg, drawing the knee forcefully back and increasing the turnout of the thigh, is stretched exactly in a straight line backwards; the right arm is raised in third position, the left one is opened in second and the head, turning to the right, is slightly raised. The torso, increasing the 'pull up', keeping the hips level and with the shoulders level, opened and lowered, is directed forward. On 1 & 2 & of the second bar, the pose is held. On 3 &, the right arm is opened in second position, the torso remains 'pulled up', the glance follows the hand and both arms are lowered simultaneously with the leg. On 4 &, the movement is concluded in the initial position. The freely lowered shoulders, the torso directed forward, the raised head with

fig. 41   *Effacée devant at 90°*

the eyes directed accordingly, impart a feeling of flight to the entire figure, giving an artistic look to the pose effacée derrière.

Pose écartée devant at 90° Initial position: fifth position, épaulement croisé, left leg in front, the arms are in the preparatory position, the head is turned to the left.

On 1 & 2 &, the arms, opening on the upbeat, are raised through the preparatory position into first simultaneously with a turn of the body to effacée; the head inclines to the left, the eyes are directed towards the hands; the working leg (the right one) is raised via the cou-de-pied derrière to the knee. On 3 & 4 &, the working leg is extended in a continuous movement in the direction of point 2 of the class diagram; the right arm is raised in third position, the left one is opened in second. The torso, increasing the 'pull up' and keeping the hips level, and with the shoulders level, opened and lowered, inclines slightly to the left; the head, turning to the right, is raised, the eyes following the right hand. On 1 & 2 & of the second bar, the pose is held. On 3 &, the right arm is opened in second position, the torso is brought upright; the head remains turned to the right and both arms are lowered simultaneously with the leg. On 4 &, the movement is concluded in fifth position, épaulement croisé, with the right leg in front (fig. 42).

The freely lowered and opened shoulders, the slightly inclined torso, the raised head and the eyes, directed towards the right hand, impart a proud carriage to the pose as well as an artistic quality.

Pose écartée derrière at 90° Initial position: fifth position, épaulement croisé, right leg in front, the arms are in preparatory position, the head is turned to the right.

On 1 & 2 &, the arms, opening on the upbeat, are raised through the preparatory position into first, simultaneously with a turn of the body to effacée; the head inclines slightly to the right, the eyes are directed towards the hands; the working leg (the right one) is raised via the conditional cou-de-pied position to the level of the knee. On 3 & 4 &, the working leg is extended in a continuous movement in the direction of point 4 of the class diagram; the right arm is raised in third position, the left one is opened in second, the head turns to the left, the eyes follow the left hand. The torso, increasing the 'pull up' and keeping the

fig. 42 Ecartée devant at 90°

shoulders and hips level, inclines slightly to the left.

On 1 & 2 & of the second bar, the pose is held. On 3 &, the right arm is opened in second position, the torso is brought upright, and both arms are lowered simultaneously with the leg. On 4 &, the movement is concluded in fifth position, épaulement croisé, with the left leg in front (fig. 43).

The freely lowered and opened shoulders, the slight inclination of the torso to the left and the eyes, directed towards the left hand, impart an artistic quality to the pose.

Remarks In the poses (particularly in the pose écartée derrière) both legs are turned out to the utmost. The torso is 'pulled up'. The working leg is opened in the pose according to the rules for battement développé, and returns to the initial position, according to the rules for battement relevé lent. The working leg may be raised above 90° according to the physical abilities of the student.

The poses at 90° are also executed with relevé lent, observing all the basic rules, and preserving the specific character of each pose.

Example 1 Pose croisée devant at 90°.

Initial position: fifth position, épaulement croisé, right leg in front, the arms are in the preparatory position, the head is turned to the right.

On 1 & 2 &, the arms, opening on the upbeat, are raised through the preparatory position into the first position, the head inclines slightly to the left, the eyes are directed towards the hands; the working leg (the right one) is stretched forward with a sliding movement. On 3 & 4 &, the working leg is raised to a height of 90° according to the rules for relevé lent. The left arm is raised in third position, the right one is opened in second, the head turns to the right, the eyes follow the right hand. The 'pull up' of the torso increases, with the shoulders level, opened and lowered. On 1 & 2 & of the second bar, the pose is held. On 3 &, the left arm is opened in second position and both arms are lowered simultaneously with the leg. On 4 &, the movement is concluded in the initial position, according to the rules for relevé lent.

fig. 43   Ecartée derrière at 90°

Example 2 Pose écartée derrière at 90°.

Initial position: fifth position, épaulement croisé, right leg in front, the arms are in the preparatory position, the head turned to the right.

On 1 & 2 &, the arms, opening on the upbeat, are raised through the preparatory position into the first position simultaneously with a turn to effacée; the head inclines slightly to the right, the eyes are directed towards the hands; the working leg is stretched forward with a sliding movement in the direction of point 4 of the class diagram. On 3 & 4 &, the working leg is raised in a continuous movement, according to the rules for relevé lent at 90° (with the turnout of both legs increasing); the right arm is raised in third position, the left one is opened in second, the head turns to the left, the eyes follow the left hand. The torso, increasing the 'pull up', keeping the shoulders and hips level, is inclined slightly to the left. On 1 & 2 & of the second bar, the pose is held. On 3 &, the right arm is opened in second position, the torso is brought upright and both arms are lowered simultaneously with the leg, according to the rules for relevé lent. On 4 &, the movement is concluded in fifth position, épaulement croisé left leg in front.

The character and time signature of the musical accompaniment are the same as those for battement développé and battement relevé lent.

Attitudes

The term attitude means the same in English as in French. As a term used in classical dance, it is applied to certain poses described below.

Attitude croisée Initial position: fifth position, épaulement croisé, left leg in front, arms in the preparatory position, head turned to the left.

On 1 & 2 & the arms, opening on the upbeat, are raised through the preparatory position into first position, the head inclines to the right, the glance is directed at the hands; the working leg (the right one) is raised via the cou-de-pied derrière to the knee. On 3 & 4 &, the working leg, drawing the knee

fig. 44   *Attitude croisée*

forcefully backwards and raising it as high as possible, is extended halfway to the back; remaining in a half-bent position. The 'pull up' of the torso increases (with the shoulders level, opened and lowered) and its unavoidable inclination is restrained, so that it remains upright. The right arm is raised in third position, the left one is opened in second. On 1 & 2 & of the second bar, the pose is held. On 3 &, the right arm is opened in second position, the right leg is stretched backwards, the 'pull up' of the torso is increased, and both arms are lowered simultaneously with the leg. On 4 &, the movement is concluded in the initial position (fig. 44).

The 'pulled up' torso, the freely opened and lowered shoulders, the active turn of the head and the focused eyes impart an artistic quality to attitude croisée, giving the entire figure a proud carriage.

Attitude effacée Initial position: fifth position, épaulement effacé, right leg behind, arms in the preparatory position, head turned to the right.

On 1 & 2 & the arms, opening on the upbeat, are raised through the preparatory position into first position, the head inclines to the left, the eyes are directed towards the hands; the working leg (the right one) is raised via the cou-de-pied derrière to the knee. On 3 & 4 &, the working leg, increasing the turnout of the upper part and drawing the knee backwards so that the entire leg is directed towards point 4 of the class diagram, begins to extend to the back, stopping in a slightly bent position. The right arm is raised in third position, the left one is opened in second; the head, turning to the right, is slightly raised. On 1 & 2 & of the second bar, the pose is held. Here it is particularly necessary to ensure that the turnout and 'lift' of the knee of the working leg are sustained; should the leg be allowed to droop, the flowing line of the entire pose would be broken. On 3 &, the right arm is opened in second position, the working leg is stretched backwards, the torso remains 'pulled up'; the head is lowered again and both arms are lowered simultaneously with the leg. On 4 &, the movement is concluded in the initial position (fig. 45).

The inclination forward of the 'pulled up' torso, keeping the shoulders and hips level, together with the soft line of the

fig. 45   Attitude effacée

working leg, should give an impression of flight. The proudly lifted head and its accompanying glance should add to this impression and impart an artistic quality to attitude effacée.

Arabesques at 90°

In the second year all four arabesques are studied, raising the leg to 90°. When first and second arabesque are executed in profile, the supporting leg assumes a half turned out position.

First arabesque Initial position: fifth position, right: leg behind. The body is directed towards point 7 of the class diagram. The arms are in preparatory position, the head is turned to the right.

On 1 & 2 &, the arms, opening on the upbeat, are raised through the preparatory position into first; the head inclines slightly to the left, the eyes are directed towards the hands. On 3 & 4 &, the right arm, beginning the movement and opening in second position, is drawn slightly to the back, the taut and turned out working leg (the right one) is extended backwards, towards point 3 of the class diagram and, without pausing on the floor, is raised to 90°. The torso resists the unavoidable inclination forward. The left arm is opened to the front, towards point 7 of the class diagram, the hands turned with palms facing down and the line of the arms softened at the elbows. The head is en face, the eyes are directed forward, continuing the line of the left arm. On 1 & 2 & of the second bar, the arabesque is held. On 3 & 4, the arms are lowered into preparatory position, the working leg, sustaining its tautness and turnout, is lowered smoothly, the torso is brought upright and the arabesque is concluded in the initial position (fig. 46).

Remarks The freely lowered and opened shoulders, the 'pulled up' though unavoidably inclined torso, the forcefully stretched legs and the softly opened arms impart a feeling of flight to first arabesque. The eyes, continuing the direction of the left arm, enhance the artistry of the pose.

Second arabesque Initial position: as described above.

On 1 & 2 &, the arms, opening on the upbeat, are raised through the preparatory position into first position, the head inclines slightly to the left, the eyes are directed towards the hands. On 3 & 4 &, the left arm, beginning the movement,

fig. 46 First arabesque

opens in second position, the taut and turned out working leg (the right one) is extended backwards towards point 3 of the class diagram and, without pausing on the floor, is raised to 90°. The torso, increasing the 'pull up', and with the left shoulder lowered, is drawn back a little, together with the arm; the spine is arched, a necessity in second arabesque. The right arm is opened forward in the direction of point 7 of the class diagram, the hands are turned with the palms facing down, the line of the arms is slightly softened at the elbows and the head turns to the right, the eye direction in harmony with the turn.

On 1 & 2 & of the second bar, the arabesque is held. On 3 & 4 &, the arms are lowered into the preparatory position; the working leg, sustaining its tautness and turnout, is lowered smoothly, the torso is brought upright and the arabesque is concluded in the initial position (fig. 47).

Remarks The torso, in spite of the arched spine and the shoulder which is drawn back, maintains its 'pull up' with the hips kept level. Both legs are taut. The turn of the head and the eyes directed to the side, which do not follow the general line of the second arabesque, produce a certain twist in the design which is characteristic of this pose.

Third arabesque Initial position: fifth position, épaulement croisé right leg in front.

On 1 & 2 &, the arms, opening on the upbeat, are raised through preparatory position into first position, the head inclines slightly to the left, the eyes are directed towards the hands. On 3 & 4 &, the right arm, beginning the movement, is opened in second position and drawn slightly backwards, the working leg (the left one) is extended backwards in the direction of point 4 of the class diagram and, without pausing on the floor, is raised, turned out and taut, to 90°. The torso maintains its 'pull up' resisting the unavoidable forward inclination. The left arm is opened to the front in the direction of point 8 of the class diagram, the hands are turned with the palms facing down; the line of the arms is softened slightly at the elbows, the head is straight with the glance directed forward, continuing the line of the left arm. On 1 & 2 & of the second bar the arabesque is held. On 3 & 4 &, the arms are lowered into the preparatory position; the working leg, remaining taut and turned out, is lowered

fig. 47   Second arabesque

smoothly, the torso is brought upright and the arabesque is concluded in the initial position (fig. 48).

Remarks The freely lowered and opened shoulders, the 'pull up' of the unavoidably inclined torso, the forcefully stretched legs and the softly opened arms impart an impetuousness to third arabesque. The eyes following the direction of the left arm enhances the artistry of the pose.

Fourth arabesque Initial position: as described above.

On 1 & 2 &, the arms, opening on the upbeat, are raised through the preparatory position into first position, the head inclines slightly to the left, the eyes are directed towards the hands. On 3 & 4 &, the left arm, beginning the movement, is opened in second position, the working leg (the left one) is extended backwards towards point 4 of the class diagram and, without pausing on the floor, is raised, turned out and taut, to 90°. The torso maintains its 'pull up'; the left shoulder, which is lowered, is drawn back together with the arm, the spine is arched, a necessity in fourth arabesque. The right arm is opened forward, towards point 8 of the class diagram; the hands are turned with the palms facing down, the line of the arms is slightly softened at the elbows, the head turns in the direction of the right arm, the eye direction is in accordance with the turn of the head. On 1 & 2 &, the arabesque is held. On 3 & 4 &, the arms are lowered into preparatory position, the working leg, remaining taut and turned out, is lowered smoothly, the torso is brought upright and the arabesque is concluded in the initial position (fig. 49).

Remarks The torso, in spite of the arched spine and the twist of the shoulders, maintains its 'pull up', and the hips are level. Both legs are stretched. The arched spine, the left shoulder drawn to the back, the turn of the head towards the right arm and the eye direction, which is in accordance with the turn of the head, produce a certain twist in the design of fourth arabesque.

The raising of the working leg in all arabesques may exceed 90° if the physical abilities of the pupils allow this.

The character and time signature of the musical accompaniment are the same as those for battement développé and battement relevé lent.

fig. 48   Third arabesque

fig. 49   Fourth arabesque

Elementary adage

At first, the poses of the classical dance, the attitudes and arabesques, are studied separately, so that the pupils master the artistic look of each pose. Afterwards the poses are combined in so-called elementary adage, which is built on a musical phrase of not less than 8–16 bars. The poses are executed not only from fifth position into fifth, but also by passing the leg from one pose to another by means of passé through first position and passé at 90°. Also included in adage are ports de bras, relevés on demi-point in the positions, and pas de bourrées. In this way co-ordination and a feeling of dance are developed. The musical accompaniment stresses the character of each included movement.

The time signature for adage is 4/4. Towards the end of the year, this can be alternated with a 6/8.

Temps lié en avant

In the second year temps lié is executed with bends of the torso.

Initial position: fifth position, épaulement croisé, right leg in front.

On the first bar, temps lié forward[1]; but on the fourth 1/4 the pose croisée derrière is held. On 1 & 2 & of the second bar, the torso, increasing the 'pull up' of the pelvic area, bends smoothly backwards at the waist starting from the upper back, the forcefully stretched legs remaining in the pose croisée derrière. On 3 &, the torso is brought upright smoothly. On 4, the left leg is closed in fifth position. On the following bar the temps lié continues to the side, but on the fourth 1/4 the left leg remains in second position with the toe pointed on the floor; the arms are opened in second position, the head is turned to the left. On 1 & 2 & of the following bar, the right arm is raised directly from second position to third; the torso, increasing the 'pull up' and keeping the weight of the body centred over the supporting leg with the hips level, is bent smoothly at the waist towards the pointed foot, the shoulders remain level, the arms remain in the same position. On 3 &, the torso is brought upright smoothly, the right arm is opened in second position, the head remains turned to the left. On 4, the left leg is closed in fifth position in

---

[1] See temps lié in the first year.

front, épaulement croisé, the arms are lowered into preparatory position and temps lié en avant is then repeated with the other leg.[2]

Temps lié en arrière

Initial position: as described above.

On the first beat: temps lié backwards[3], but on the fourth 1/4 the pose croisée devant is held. On 1 & 2 & of the second bar the torso, increasing the 'pull up' of the pelvic area, bends smoothly backwards at the waist starting from the upper back, the forcefully stretched legs remain in the pose croisée devant. On 3 &, the torso is brought upright smoothly. On 4, the right leg is closed in fifth position. On the following bar, temps lié to the side, but on the fourth 1/4 the right leg remains in second position with the toe pointed on the floor, the arms are opened in second position and the head is turned to the left. On 1 & 2 & of the following bar, the right arm is raised directly from second position to third position; the torso, increasing the 'pull up' and keeping the weight of the body centred over the supporting leg with the hips level, bends smoothly at the waist to the left. The shoulders remain level and the arms remain in the same position. On 3 &, the torso is brought upright smoothly, the right arm is opened in second position and the head remains turned to the left. On 4, the right leg is closed in fifth position behind, épaulement croisé; the arms are lowered in preparatory position and then temps lié derrière is repeated with the other leg.

Remarks The flow and smoothness of the execution, keeping the weight of the body centred over the supporting leg during the bends, are very important in temps lié.

The time signature is 4/4 or 3/4. The character of the musical accompaniment is legato.

Fourth port de bras

Initial position: fifth position, épaulement croisé, right leg in front.

---

[2] As in temps lié the functions of the working leg and the supporting leg are alternated constantly, we will speak of the right and left leg. Where necessary it will be indicated which leg is the supporting one.

[3] *See* temps lié in the first year.

Two introductory chords: on the first chord the arms are raised through the preparatory position into first position; on the second the left arm is raised in third position, the right one is opened in second position and the head turns to the right. On the upbeat, on &, the turned head is raised[1], the eyes are directed towards the left hand; both arms, maintaining their positions, are lengthened, beginning at the fingertips. On 1 & 2 &, the left arm is lowered in second position, the palms of the hands are gradually turned downwards, the elbows are slightly softened and the freely opened and lowered shoulders are turned on 3 &; the left one to the back and the right one to the front, so that the arms, continuing the line of the shoulders, are placed diagonally; the head turns to the right. The shoulders, arms and head take an active part in the movement. The legs, in fifth position, and the hips, in épaulement croisé, remain immobile. On 4 &, the torso, increasing the 'pull up' and keeping the hips level, bends gradually slightly backwards at the waist starting from the upper back: the shoulders, arms and head remain in the same positions. On 1 & 2 & of the following bar, the shoulders return to the initial position, the arms are joined in first position, the head inclines to the left. On 3 & 4 &, the left arm is raised in third position, the right one is opened in second, the head turns to the right. '&' is the upbeat for the repeat of the port de bras.

Remarks In fourth port de bras one should achieve an even, fluent execution. The shoulders are firmly lowered, especially the one which is drawn to the back; and the forcefully stretched legs maintain an exact fifth position in épaulement croisé (fig. 50).

Fifth port de bras

Initial position: fifth position, épaulement croisé, right leg in front.

Two introductory chords: on the first one the arms are raised in first position, on the second one the left arm is raised in third position, the right one is opened in second, the head turns to the right.

---

[1] In order to avoid a strained neck or a backward drop of the head, the movement is executed with a slight raise of the chin.

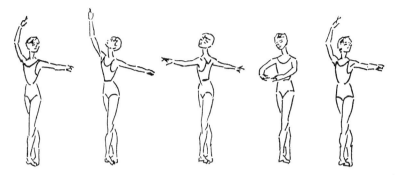

fig. 50   Fourth port de bras

On the upbeat on &, the head is turned and raised[1], the eyes
are directed towards the left hand, both arms are opened
slightly, starting the movement at the fingertips, as if lengthening the movement. On 1 & 2 &, the torso, with the legs and hips
particularly 'pulled up', bends smoothly forward, and the arms
are joined in first position, (the left one being lowered and the
right one being raised through the preparatory position). The
head is lowered, the eyes are directed towards the hands. On 3
&, the torso, which is now upright, is turned slightly to the left;
the legs and hips remain immobile in fifth position, the arms
remain in first position. On 4 &, the torso, with the shoulders
level, opened and lowered, bends smoothly backwards at the
waist, starting from the upper back; the right arm is raised in
third position, the left one is opened in second, the head turns to
the left. On 1 & 2 & of the second bar, the torso continues to
bend, the right arm is opened in second position, the left one is
closed in third, the head turns to the right. On 3 & 4 &, the torso,
which has been brought smoothly upright, returns to the initial
position. '&' is the upbeat for the repeat.

Remarks The execution of fifth port de bras demands an uninterrupted flow. The arms and head should be totally free from
tension during the bend of the torso.

The character and time signature of the musical accompani-

---

[1] *See* footnote for fourth port de bras.

ment are the same as in the preceding ports de bras. Initially fifth port de bras is studied taking two bars of 4/4.

Pas de bourrée de côté

Initial position: fifth position, épaulement croisé, right foot in front.

Préparation on two introductory chords. On the first chord, the arms, opening on the upbeat, are brought to the raised preparatory position, the head inclines to the left shoulder, the eyes are directed at the hands. On the second chord, while turning en face, the right leg executes demi plié, the left one is stretched to the side at 45°, passing with a fleeting movement through cou-de-pied derrière. The arms, preserving their curve, are opened in the direction of second position, the head turns to the left.

On 1, the left leg, sliding with the toe along the floor, goes onto a high demi-point behind the right leg, as if replacing it; the right leg is raised immediately to the conditional cou-de-pied position, the arms are raised through the preparatory position into first position, the head turns en face. On 2, the right leg, opening, transfers to a high demi-point in the direction of second position, the left leg is raised sur le cou-de-pied derrière, the positions of arms and head are held. On 3, the left leg executes a demi plié, the right one is stretched to the side at 45°, passing with a fleeting movement through the conditional cou-de-pied position. The arms, preserving their curve, are opened at half height in second position, the head turns to the right, the eyes are directed at the right hand. On 4, the position is held. On 1 of the second bar, the right leg, sliding with the toe along the floor, goes onto a high demi-point in front of the left leg, as if replacing it; the left leg is raised sur le cou-de-pied derrière, the arms are raised through the preparatory position into first position, the head turns en face. On 2, the left leg, opening, transfers onto high demi-point, in the direction of second position; the right one is raised immediately to the conditional cou-de-pied position, the positions of head and arms are held. On 3, the right leg executes a demi plié, the left one is stretched to the side at 45°, passing with a fleeting movement through cou-de-pied derrière; the arms are opened in second position at half height, the head turns to the left and the eyes are directed towards the left hand. On 4, the position is held. The pas de bourrée is executed the required number of times. On two concluding chords the movement is ended in the initial position. Having mastered pas de bourrée de côté, one proceeds to study it in the poses écartée devant and derrière.

Pas de bourrée ballotté in effacée

Pas de bourrée ballotté is executed in the poses croisée and effacée. The arms are the same as in the small poses, with the exception of pas de bourrée effacée derrière. The change of arms in pas de bourrée effacée derrière accentuates the active participation of the torso in this movement.

Initial position: fifth position, épaulement croisé, right leg in front. The anacrusis is divided into 3/8. On the first 1/8 the arms are opened; on the second they close and are then raised in the raised first position, the head inclining to the left, the eyes directed towards the hands. On the third 1/8 the right leg executes a demi plié, the left one is raised sur le cou-de-pied derrière; the arms, preserving their curve, are opened in the direction of second position and the head turns to the right.

On 1, with a change of direction to épaulement effacé, the left leg goes onto a high demi-point behind the right one as if replacing it, the right leg, increasing the turnout of the thigh, is raised immediately to the conditional cou-de-pied position. The arms are raised through the preparatory position into first position, the head turns to the left. On 2, the right leg, opening in the direction of point 2 of the class diagram, transfers to a high demi-point; the left one is raised sur le cou-de-pied derrière, the positions of head and arms are held. On 3, the left leg executes a demi plié, the right one is stretched to effacée devant with the toe on the floor, passing with a fleeting move-ment through the conditional cou-de-pied position; the right arm is opened in second position, the left one remains in first position, the head remains turned to the left; the 'pulled up' torso, with the shoulders level, inclines backwards. On 4, the position is held and on the second bar, the pas de bourrée is executed to the back.

On 1 of the second bar, the right leg, sliding with the toe along the floor, steps onto a high demi-point in front of the left leg as if replacing it; the left leg is raised sur le cou-de-pied derrière. The right arm is united with the left one in first position, the head inclines slightly to the left, the glance is directed at the hands. On 2, the left leg, opening in the direction of point 6 of the class diagram, transfers to a high demi-point, the right one is raised to the conditional cou-de-pied position; the positions of arms and head are held. On 3, the right leg executes a demi plié, the left one opens to effacée derrière, with the toe on the floor, passing it with a fleeting movement through cou-de-pied derrière. The left arm is opened in second position, the right one remains in first; the 'pulled up' torso, with the shoulders level, inclines forward, the head and the focus are directed forward, thus continuing the line of the torso. On 4, the position is held.

Pas de bourrée ballotté is ended on two concluding chords.

Remarks Pas de bourrée ballotté is executed briskly and energetically. The supporting leg as well as the working one remain fully turned out in all positions. The torso is 'pulled up', the supporting leg is taut, the instep and toes of the working leg are stretched, particularly sur le cou-de-pied. The arms are fixed accurately, both in first position and in the poses.

After mastering pas de bourrée ballotté in all directions, it can be executed combining several directions and poses.

The character of the musical accompaniment is brisk and energetic. The time signature is 4/4. Later it changes to 3/4. In this case, the poses at the end of each movement are not held, the pas de bourrée beginning immediately in the opposite direction.

Allegro

In jumps, the épaulement position changes its direction slightly. In fifth position, épaulement croisé, right foot in front, the direction shifts a little from point 8 towards point 1 of the class diagram. In fifth position, épaulement croisé, left foot in front, from point 2 towards point 1. The active turn of the head is preserved. This enables one to execute the jumps forcefully and correctly and facilitates the transition en face at the beginning of the jump and its conclusion in épaulement.

The demi plié also changes, in that it becomes shorter and

more springy. The jumping exercises in the first year develop the strength and the resilience of the muscles. In the second year the height of the jump is increased and the muscles are trained in small jumps.

Grand changement de pieds

Initial position: fifth position, épaulement croisé, right foot in front.

The anacrusis is divided into 2/8. On the first 1/8, demi plié in fifth position. On the second 1/8, the legs push forcefully away from the floor, fixing fifth position en face in a high jump. As a result of the jump in the air, the legs are stretched to the utmost, increasing the turnout and resisting the pull of gravity; they change, opening only to the extent that one leg does not touch the other. On 1 &, the legs, moving from the toes through the whole foot, alight in fifth position in demi plié, and changement de pieds is concluded in épaulement croisé, left leg in front. On 2, the knees are straightened slowly. On 3, a pause; 4 is the plié for the following changement de pieds (fig. 51).

Petit changement de pieds

Initial position: fifth position, épaulement croisé, right leg in front.

The anacrusis is divided into 2/8. On the first 1/8, demi plié in fifth position. On the second 1/8, the legs push away from the floor, sustaining fifth position en face in the air in a low jump and without delaying, increasing the turnout, they change,

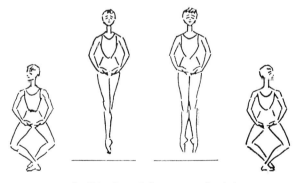

fig. 51   Grand changement de pieds

123

opening only to the extent that one leg does not touch the other. On 1, the legs, moving from the toes through the whole foot, alight in fifth position demi plié, and changement de pieds is concluded in épaulement croisé, left leg in front. On 2, the knees are straightened slowly. On 3 a pause; 4 is the plié for the following changement de pieds.

Remarks In fifth position demi plié the heels must be pressed firmly into the floor while the legs are turned out completely. In the jump the legs are stretched to the utmost. It is extremely important to remember this in petit changement de pieds, in order to be able to stretch the knees, insteps and toes forcefully within the space of a short, low jump. The torso is forcefully 'pulled up'. The arms, in the preparatory position, are held without strain.

The time signature is 4/4. At first, changement de pieds is executed with one jump to the bar; later on, one jump on each 1/4, at least eight times consecutively. The character of the musical accompaniment is brisk and energetic.

Pas glissade

Glissade (slide): its character precludes a high jump.

Initial position: fifth position, épaulement croisé, right leg in front.

On 1, demi plié in fifth position with the torso 'pulled up'. On 2, turning en face, the right leg is stretched with a sliding movement to the side, at the same time the knee, instep and toes of the left leg are forcefully stretched in a sharp jump; for a moment one should see the legs in second position in the air. On 3, the left leg is closed in fifth position behind, with a sliding movement, and demi plié is executed on the spot which was marked by the pointed toes of the right leg. On 4, the legs are straightened in épaulement croisé, right leg in front. In glissade with the right leg, the head remains turned to the right, with the left leg, to the left. During the execution of glissade the arms remain in a free and easy preparatory position.

Glissade travelling to the side can also begin with the back foot: the head remains turned towards the front foot. Later on consecutive glissades in a sideways direction are executed with a change of the legs, the turn of the head changing with the changing of the feet in fifth position. Later still, the arms are included in the movement.

On 1, the arms, opening on the upbeat, are brought together in the raised preparatory position simultaneously with demi plié in fifth position. On 2, the arms are opened in the direction of second position while fixing the position of the legs in the jump. On 3 & 4, the arms are closed in the preparatory position.

At first glissade is studied en face forwards, to the side and backwards. Later on, glissades forwards and backwards are executed in the small poses croisée and effacée.

Example Glissade in the pose croisée devant.

Initial position: fifth position, épaulement croisé, right foot in front.

On 1, demi plié in fifth position; the arms, opening on the upbeat, are raised in first position, the head inclines to the left, the eyes are directed towards the hands. On 2, while fixing fourth position of the legs in the jump, the right arm is opened in second position, the left one remains in first position, the head turns to the right (small pose croisée). This position is sustained during the given number of glissades. On the last glissade, the arms are lowered in preparatory position.

Remarks It is recommended to begin the study of pas glissade to the side facing the barre. In this case the arms, maintaining their position opposite the centre of the torso, slide along the barre during the jump. During the execution of glissade the torso is 'pulled up', the knees, insteps and toes are stretched to the utmost, while the jump is fixed in the air.

The time signature is 4/4. At first, each glissade is executed in one bar; later on, each one takes 1/4. The character of the musical accompaniment is brisk and energetic.

Grand et petit echappé

Grand et petit échappé, just as changement de pieds, develop the height of the jump and train the leg muscles.

Grand échappé Initial position: fifth position, épaulement croisé, right foot in front.

The anacrusis is divided into three 1/8. On the first 1/8, the arms are slightly opened; on the second 1/8, demi plié in fifth position, the arms are closed in preparatory position. On the third 1/8, the legs push forcefully away from the floor, fixing fifth position en face in the air in a high jump; the arms are raised in first position.

On 1, the fully stretched legs, resisting the pull of gravity, open and come down in second position demi plié; the arms are opened in second position, the head turns to the right. On &, the legs, without relaxing the muscles, push forcefully away from the floor, fixing second position en face in the air in a high jump; the arms and head are held in the same position. On 2 &, the fully stretched legs, resisting the pull of gravity, are joined together in the air in fifth position (the left leg in front) and come down gradually in demi plié in fifth position, épaulement croisé; the arms are closed in preparatory position, the head turns to the left. On 3 &, the knees are straightened, concluding échappé. 4 is the plié for the following échappé.

Petit échappé Initial position: as described above.

The anacrusis is divided into three 1/8. On the first 1/8 the arms are opened slightly; on the second 1/8, demi plié in fifth position, the arms are closed in preparatory position. On the third 1/8, the legs push away from the floor, fixing fifth position en face in the air in a low jump, the arms are brought to the raised preparatory position. On 1, the legs open and come down in second position demi plié; the arms are opened in the direction of second position, the head turns to the right. On &, the legs, without relaxing the muscles, push away from the floor, stretching to the utmost in second position in the air; the arms and head are held in the same positions. On 2 &, the legs come down in demi plié in fifth position, épaulement croisé (left leg in front); the arms are closed in preparatory position, the head turns to the left. On 3 &, the knees are straightened, concluding échappé. 4 is the plié for the following échappé.

Remarks In demi plié in fifth and second positions, the heels are pressed firmly into the floor with the legs completely turned out. In the jump the legs are stretched to the utmost: it is particularly important to remember this in petit échappé, in order to be able to stretch the legs during the short, low jump. The torso is always 'pulled up' and easy, which helps the jump. The arms execute the movements freely.

The character of the musical accompaniment is brisk and energetic.

Jeté in the small poses

Initial position: fifth position, épaulement croisé, left leg in front.

The anacrusis is divided into three 1/8. On the first 1/8, the arms are opened slightly. On the second 1/8, demi plié in fifth position, bringing the arms to the raised preparatory position. On the third 1/8, while turning en face, the right leg is opened in second position with a brushing movement; simultaneously with a vertical jump of the left leg, the arms are opened in second position. On 1 &, the right leg comes down in demi plié, replacing the left leg; the left leg is bent sur le cou-de-pied derrière, the right arm is closed in first position. The left arm remains in second, the head turns to the right. On 2 &, the right leg is straightened, the left leg is lowered in fifth position behind, the arms are lowered in preparatory position. On 3 &, the position is held. On 4, demi plié in fifth position, and execute jeté with the other leg.

Jeté in the small poses in the opposite direction Initial position: fifth position épaulement croisé, right leg in front.

The upbeat is divided into three 1/8. On the first 1/8, the arms are opened. On the second 1/8, demi plié in fifth position, bringing the arms to the raised preparatory position. On the third 1/8, while turning en face, the right leg is opened in second position, with a brushing movement; simultaneously with a vertical jump of the left leg, the arms are opened in second position. On 1 &, the right leg comes down in demi plié, replacing the left leg, the left leg is bent in the conditional cou-de-pied position, the right arm is closed in first position, the left arm remains in second and the head turns to the left. On 2 &, the right leg is straightened, the left leg is lowered in fifth position in front, the arms are lowered into preparatory position. On 3 &, the position is held. On 4, demi plié in fifth position and execute jeté with the other leg.

After mastering jeté in the small poses with a pause, it is

executed without pausing, initially no more than twice in succession.

In consecutive jetés, the leg which is sur le cou-de-pied is at first lowered into fifth position and then, with a brushing movement, is opened in second position at 45°. Later on, the leg is thrown out at 45° immediately from the cou-de-pied, simultaneously with the jump onto the other leg. In both cases the arms are opened in second position when the legs are completely stretched and turned out in the air. At the conclusion of the jeté the arms assume the small pose.

The time signature is 4/4 at first; later on it is 2/4. The character of the music is the same as in the first year.

Pas échappé onto one leg
Initial position: fifth position épaulement croisé, right leg in front.

The anacrusis is divided into three 1/8. On the first 1/8, the arms are opened slightly. On the second 1/8, demi plié in fifth position, the arms return to preparatory position. On the third 1/8, the legs push away from the floor, fixing fifth position en face in the air in a high jump, raising the arms in first position. On 1, the extremely stretched legs, resisting the force of gravity, open and come down in demi plié in second position; the arms are opened in second position, the head turning to the right. On &, the legs, without relaxing the muscles, push away from the floor, fixing second position in a high jump; the arms and head remain in the same positions. On 2 &, the left leg, resisting the force of gravity, comes down in demi plié, with the right one bent sur le cou-de-pied derrière; the right arm is closed through the preparatory position into first position, the left one remaining in second, the head turns to the left. On 3 &, both legs conclude the échappé in fifth position, épaulement croisé. The arms are closed in preparatory position. 4 is the plié for the execution of the following échappé, with the other leg.

Pas échappé onto one leg in the opposite direction Initial position: fifth position épaulement croisé, right leg in front.

The upbeat is divided into three 1/8. On the first 1/8, the arms are opened slightly. On the second 1/8, demi plié in fifth position, the arms returning to the preparatory position. On the third 1/8, the legs push away from the floor, fixing fifth position en face in the air in a high jump. The arms are raised in first position. On 1, the fully stretched legs, resisting the force of gravity, open and come down in demi plié in second position; the arms are opened in second position, the head turns to the right. On &, the legs, without relaxing the muscles, push away from the floor, fixing second position in a high jump. The arms and head remain in the same positions. On 2 &, the right leg, resisting the force of gravity, comes down in demi plié, with the left leg bent in the conditional cou-de-pied position; the right arm is closed in first position, the left arm remains in second, the head turns to the left. On 3 &, both legs conclude the échappé in fifth position, épaulement croisé, with the arms closing into the preparatory position. 4 is the plié for the execution of the following échappé, with the other leg.

The time signature and character of the musical accompaniment are the same as in grand échappé.

Pas assemblé in poses

The study of pas assemblé in poses is commenced when this movement has been mastered en face to the front, to the side and to the back.

In assemblé to the front and to the back, the leg, maintaining the turnout, is opened exactly in a straight line; the legs are brought together in fifth position in the air; the arms remain at ease in the preparatory position.

In assemblé in poses, the arms assume the small pose on two introductory chords; they remain completely free and without strain during the jump. The leg opens precisely in the directions croisée or effacée, especially in assemblé derrière.

The torso is 'pulled up', during the jump as well as in the following demi plié. On two concluding chords, the arms are lowered into the preparatory position, one from first position, the other one directly from second. Later on the pose is assumed during the jump, instead of beforehand.

Example Assemblé in the pose croisée devant.

Initial position: fifth position, épaulement croisé, right leg in front.

On 1, demi plié in fifth position, bringing the arms to the raised preparatory position, inclining the head to the left, with the eyes directed at the hands. On &, the jump: the right arm is opened in second position, the left one remains in first, the head turns to the right. On 2 &, the assemblé is concluded in demi plié in fifth position. On 3 &, the knees are straightened. On 4 &, the pose croisée is held, and the assemblé is then repeated. At the conclusion of the exercise the arms are lowered in preparatory position simultaneously with the demi plié of the last assemblé.

Assemblés in the pose croisée derrière and in the poses effacée devant and derrière are executed according to the same rules, keeping in mind the particular characteristics of each pose.

The time signature is 4/4, each movement is executed in one bar. Later on the time signature is 2/4 and the movement now begins on the upbeat.

> *Example* The upbeat is divided into three 1/8. On the first 1/8, the arms are opened. On the second 1/8, demi plié in fifth position, bringing the arms to the raised preparatory position; on the third 1/8 assemblé in the small pose.

At first the assemblé is executed separately, each movement in one bar; later on, each movement on 1/4.

Double assemblé

Double assemblé is executed with the same leg twice. When double assemblé is executed to the side the legs do not change position in the first assemblé; when changing position in the second assemblé, the head is also turned. The rules of execution are the same as for assemblé, only the second assemblé is executed more actively.

The musical accompaniment is the same as for assemblé.

Pas de basque

Pas de basque is literally a step from the national dances of the Spanish Basques. This movement also occurs in many other national dances. In the classical dance it is stylised. It is one of the most complicated jumps from the syllabus of the second year. It cultivates a feeling for dance as well as movement co-ordination. Like glissade, pas de basque has a sliding character and therefore a high jump is excluded.

Pas de basque en avant Initial position: fifth position épaulement croisé, right foot in front.

The upbeat is divided into three 1/8. On the first 1/8, demi plié in fifth position; the arms, having been opened, return to the preparatory position. On the second 1/8 the right leg is stretched, with a sliding movement in the direction of point 8 of the class diagram; the arms are raised in first position, the head inclines to the left, the eyes are directed at the hands. On the third 1/8, the stretched right leg, sliding with the toe along the floor, describes a semi-circle to second position. The left one, remaining in demi plié, turns en face; the arms are opened in second position, the head turns to the left and immediately the knee, instep and toes of the left leg are forcefully stretched in a short jump. On 1, while the torso and legs turn towards point 2 of the class diagram, the legs are brought together in first position, demi plié, on the spot indicated by the pointed toe of the right leg. The arms are closed in preparatory position, the head is lowered and inclines to the right, the eyes follow the left hand. On &, the left leg is stretched, with a sliding movement in the direction of point 2 of the class diagram, the right one remains in demi plié, the arms are raised in first position, the eyes are directed towards the hands. On 2, the left leg, sliding with the toe along the floor, extends the movement and transfers to demi plié, the right one is straightened behind, touching the floor with pointed toes; the 'pulled up' torso is sent forward, the arms maintain the same position. On &, the left leg jumps up and is joined immediately by the right one in fifth position in the air. On 3 &, travelling slightly forward, the legs come smoothly down in fifth position demi plié (left leg in front); the arms are opened, the head inclines to the left, the eyes are directed towards the left hand. On 1 & of the second bar, the legs are straightened, the arms are lowered in preparatory position, the head turns to the left and pas de basque is concluded in épaulement croisé, with the left leg in front. On 2 & 3, the pose is held.

Pas de basque en arrière Initial position: fifth position épaulement croisé, right leg behind.

The anacrusis is divided into three 1/8. On the first 1/8, demi plié in fifth position; the arms, having been opened, return to the preparatory position. On the second 1/8, the right leg is stretched, with a sliding movement, in the direction of point 6 of the class diagram; the arms are raised in first position, the head inclines to the right, the eyes are directed at the hands. On the third 1/8, the stretched right leg, sliding with the toe along the floor, describes a semicircle to second position; the left one, remaining in demi plié, sends the heel forward, turning en face. The arms are opened in second position, the head turns to the right and immediately the knee, instep and toes of the left leg are forcefully stretched in a short jump. On 1, while the torso and the legs turn towards point 8 of the class diagram, the legs are brought together in first position, demi plié, on the spot indicated by the pointed toe of the right leg. The arms are closed in preparatory position, the head is lowered and inclines to the left, the eyes follow the right hand. On &, the left leg is stretched with a sliding movement in the direction of point 4 of the class diagram, the right one remains in demi plié, the arms are raised in first position, the eyes are directed towards the hands. On 2, the left leg, sliding with the toe along the floor, extends the movement and transfers to demi plié; the right one is straightened in front, touching the floor with pointed toes; the 'pulled up' torso is sent backwards with a slight backbend, the arms remaining in the same position. On &, the left leg jumps up and is joined immediately by the right one, in fifth position in the air. On 3 &, travelling slightly backwards, the legs come down smoothly in fifth position demi plié, the left leg behind; the arms are opened, the head inclines to the right, the eyes are directed towards the right hand. On 1 & of the second bar, the legs are straightened, the arms are lowered in preparatory position, the head turns to the right and pas de basque is concluded in épaulement croisé, with the left leg behind. On 2 & 3 &, the position is held.

Remarks The execution of pas de basque should be flowing, and fully turned out in all positions. The 'pulled up' torso and the exact co-ordination of arms and head impart a lightness to this step.

The musical beat is 3/4. The character is that of a slow Mazurka. At first, pas de basque takes two bars: the first bar for the pas de basque itself; at the beginning of the second bar, the position is held, the last three 1/8 of the second bar being used as the anacrusis for the following pas de basque. When this has been mastered, pas de basque is executed in one bar: the demi plié at the end of the first pas de basque is on the count of 3; '&' is the upbeat for the following pas de basque.

Sissonne ouverte

Sissonne ouverte is an open jump. In the first half of the year it is executed with the toes of the extended leg touching the floor; in the second half of the year, with the leg at 45°. In both cases, the study of sissonne ouverte is begun to the side.

Initial position: fifth position épaulement croisé, right leg in front.

On 1, the arms, opening on the upbeat, are closed in preparatory position, together with a demi plié in fifth position. On &, the legs push forcefully away from the floor, stretching the knees, instep and toes in a high jump en face. On 2, the left leg comes down in demi plié, the right one, sustaining the turnout, is opened through the conditional cou-de-pied position, into second position with the toes on the floor. On &, the left leg forcefully pushes away from the floor, jumping up, and is joined by the right one in fifth position in the air, left leg in front. On 3 &, the legs, transferring through the toes to the whole foot, come down in fifth position in demi plié, and the sissonne ouverte is concluded in épaulement croisé, with the left leg in front. On 4 & the knees are straightened and the movement is then continued with the other leg (fig. 52).

Later on movements of arms and head are included; the arms, opening on the upbeat, are brought to the raised preparatory

fig. 52   Sissonne ouverte

133

position at the moment of the jump with the torso and head turned en face; the arms are opened in the direction of second position simultaneously with the working leg; the head inclines to the left[1], the eyes are directed towards the right hand. At the conclusion of the movement, the arms are lowered in preparatory position and the head turns to the left. In sissonne ouverte to the side in the opposite direction, the leg, opening from fifth position behind, goes to second position through the conditional cou-de-pied derrière, the arms are opened in second position, the head turns towards the opened leg in profile, that is without inclining.

Having mastered sissonne ouverte to the side, it is executed forwards and backwards, en face. In sissonne ouverte forwards and backwards, the leg is opened exactly in a straight line, shoulders and hips remaining level. The arms, being brought to the raised preparatory position at the moment of the jump, are opened in the direction of second position simultaneously with the working leg, towards which the head turns. Simultaneously with the demi plié in fifth position, the arms are lowered into preparatory position.

Remarks Sissonne ouverte in all directions is executed with a 'pulled up', light torso and well turned out legs. The arms are opened in second position at the level of the raised preparatory position.

The time signature is 4/4. The movement is executed in one bar. The character of the musical accompaniment is energetic and precise.

Sissonne fermée

The initial position of sissonne fermée, a closed jump, is fifth position, épaulement croisé, right leg in front.

On 1, the arms, opening on the upbeat, are closed in preparatory position, simultaneously with the demi plié in fifth position. On &, the legs push forcefully away from the floor, opening in second position at 45° in a vertical jump, travelling towards point 3 of the class diagram. On 2 &, the legs, without relaxing the muscles, conclude the jump on the spot indicated by the pointed

---

[1] When executing sissonne ouverte with the right leg.

fig. 53   Sissonne fermée

toes of the right leg, closing simultaneously in fifth position demi plié, right leg in front. On 3 & 4 &, the legs are straightened in the initial position. In sissonne fermée, the torso is 'pulled up' and light, the arms maintain an easy preparatory position, the head is turned to the right[1].

Having mastered sissonne fermée travelling in the direction of the front leg, one proceeds to the study of sissonne fermée towards the back leg. Later on sissonne fermée is executed consecutively in one direction, changing the legs after the jump, the head turning towards the leg which is in front at the conclusion of the jump. At first sissonne fermée is executed with the arms in the preparatory position; later on the arms accompany the movement. On 1, the arms, opening on the upbeat, are brought to the raised preparatory position simultaneously with the demi plié in fifth position. On &, the arms are opened, during the jump, in the direction of second position; on 2, the arms are closed in preparatory position, together with demi plié in fifth position (fig. 53).

Remarks At the beginning of the jump, an active part should be played by the leg in the direction of which one is travelling. At the end of the jump, when the legs close in demi plié, an active part is played by the other leg: quickly sliding with the toe along the floor, it finishes the jump almost simultaneously with the other leg.

---

[1] In sissonne fermée the head is always turned towards the leg which is in front at the conclusion of the jump.

Time signature 4/4: 2/4 of the bar for the jump, 2/4 to pause. Later on, 1/4 of a bar for the jump, 1/4 to pause. Later still, sissonne fermée is executed taking 1/4 of a bar each. The character of the music is energetic and precise.

Movements for the stage

Besides studying the movements in their academic form, some theatrical forms of the same movements are studied in class, e.g. theatrical préparation, theatrical sissonne in first arabesque and theatrical pas de chat (usually combined with theatrical sissonne in first arabesque).

Préparation
Initial position: fifth position épaulement croisé, right leg in front.

On 1, demi plié with the right leg, the left one is raised sur le cou-de-pied derrière; the arms opening slightly on the upbeat, are raised through the preparatory position into first, the head inclines slightly to the left, the eyes are directed towards the hands. On &, the left leg is stretched to the back, with the toe on the floor in croisé. On 2, the left leg, executing a step backwards, is placed on the floor, the right leg is stretched croisé devant touching the floor with pointed toes and the arms are opened slightly, the head turning to the right.

Sissonne in first arabesque
Initial position: fifth position épaulement croisé, right leg in front.

The anacrusis is divided into two 1/8. On the first 1/8, with a turn towards point 3 of the class diagram, the arms, opening slightly, are raised through the preparatory position into first, the head inclines slightly, with the eyes directed towards the hands. On the second 1/8 the right leg, sliding with the toe along the floor in the direction of point 3 of the class diagram, transfers to demi plié and immediately on 1, it pushes away from the floor; in the jump, the leg is raised a little, the arms are opened in a high first arabesque, the head is raised and the eyes are directed towards the right hand. On 2 & 3, the jump is concluded in demi plié, holding the arabesque. On 1 of the second bar, the right leg is straightened; on 2, the left one is closed in fifth position in front, with a turn towards point 7 of the class diagram, and the arms are lowered into the preparatory position. On 3, the left leg slides in the direction of point 7 and the movement is repeated to the other side (fig. 54).

*fig. 54
Sissonne in
first arabesque*

Remarks Theatrical sissonne in first arabesque differs somewhat from the conventional first arabesque in class. The fully raised torso, the raised arm, continuing the line of the torso, and the eyes, following the hand, give the jump a light and flying character.

The arms, opening in arabesque, pass clearly through the preparatory position into first. The supporting leg, forcefully pushing away from the floor, must be fully stretched at the moment of the jump.

The theatrical sissonne is executed combined with pas de chat and balancé.

The time signature is 3/4. A fast waltz.

Sissonne in first arabesque combined with pas de chat On the first bar, theatrical sissonne is executed on the right leg, concluding in first arabesque. On 1 of the second bar, the left leg, coming down, is brought to fifth position in front in demi plié; the right leg is raised sur le cou-de-pied derrière, the arms are lowered into the preparatory position with the head inclining slightly. On 2, the right leg unfolds a little, simultaneously with a jump of the left leg, it is then brought foward, coming down in demi plié, and the left leg (as if catching up with the right one) comes down through the conditional cou-de-pied position into fifth. The arms are raised in first position, the eyes are directed towards the hands. On 3, without delaying after the pas de chat, the right leg is stretched forward, beginning the sissonne in arabesque as the combination is repeated.

Remarks Theatrical sissonne combined with pas de chat is executed on a straight line from point 7 towards point 3 of the class diagram and vice versa, as well as on the diagonal, from point 6 towards point 2 of the class diagram with the right leg, and from point 4 towards point 8 of the class diagram with the left one. Having mastered sissonne in first arabesque, it is preceded by the theatrical préparation, which is exectued on two introductory chords or on the upbeat.

Exercices sur les pointes

In exercises on point the épaulement position, as in jumps, slightly alters its direction (see allegro).

Echappé with relevé on point in second position
Initial position: fifth position épaulement croisé, right leg in front.

On the upbeat, demi plié in fifth position, bringing the arms to the raised preparatory position. On 1 &, with a turn en face, the legs, opening simultaneously and evenly, rise on point in second position. The arms are opened in the direction of second position, the eyes are directed towards the right hand. On 2 &, the legs, increasing the turnout, come down in demi plié in second position, the positions of arms and head are held. On 3 &, relevé on point in second position, the hands are opened slightly. On 4 &, the legs are closed in fifth position, demi plié, épaulement croisé, left leg in front; the head turns to the left, the arms are closed in the preparatory position and échappé is then continued with the other leg. Relevé on point in second position can be executed four times or more.

Remarks During the execution of échappé the legs are turned out and the torso is 'pulled up', facilitating the relevé on point. The movements of the arms and the turns of the head are free and without strain.

The character of the musical accompaniment is precise and energetic The time signature is 4/4. At first, échappé with relevé on point is executed in two bars. One bar: échappé with relevé on point; the second bar: a pause. Later on, échappé with relevé on point is executed without pausing. Later still, on 1/8. Demi plie on the upbeat; on 1, second position on point; on &, demi plié; 2 is the second position on point; on &, demi plié in second position; 3 is the second position on point; on &, demi plié in fifth position, on 4, straighten the legs.

Relevé on point in fourth position
Relevé on point in fourth position consolidates the correct position of torso and legs at the moment of relevé.

Initial position: fifth position, épaulement croisé, right leg in front.

Two introductory chords. On 1 &, with a turn en face, the right leg executes battement tendu to the front. On 2 &, the heel is lowered in fourth position en face, the arms remain in the preparatory position and the head is turned to the right. On the upbeat, demi plié in fourth position. On 1, relevé on point. On 2 &, demi plié in fourth position etc. until the end of the musical phrase. On two concluding chords, the right leg returns to fifth position, épaulement croisé, according to the rules for battement tendu. Having mastered relevé on point in fourth position en face, it is studied in épaulement croisé and effacé.

Remarks In relevé on point the legs maintain the turnout in demi plié as well as on point, the weight of the body is distributed evenly over both legs; shoulders and hips are level.

Pas sus-sous
Pas sus-sous is executed according to the rules for relevé on point in fifth position, travelling forwards and backwards. When travelling forwards, an active part is played by the leg which is in fifth position behind, as if it were pushing the other leg forward. When travelling backwards, an active part is played by the leg which is in fifth position in front, as if it were pulling the other leg back. Travelling in either direction, the legs must maintain an absolutely tight fifth position.

The positions of the arms can be varied: they can be either in the small and big poses croisée and effacée, or both arms can be in third position.

When combining pas sus-sous with other movements, the time signature and character of the music are determined by these movements.

Pas de bourrée on point

Pas de bourrée on point, with and without a change of the legs, in all directions and poses, is executed according to the rules for pas de bourrée on demi-point.

The musical accompaniment is the same as in the first year.

Assemblé soutenu

Initial position: fifth position épaulement croisé, right leg in front; the arms are in the preparatory position, the head is turned to the right.

On 1, demi plié in fifth position; the arms, opening slightly on the upbeat, are brought to the raised preparatory position. On &, with a turn en face, the left leg is stretched with a sliding movement to second position, the arms are opened in second position, the head turns to the left. On 2, the left leg, sliding with pointed toes, is pulled towards the right one and both legs are joined together simultaneously in fifth position on point, left leg in front; the arms return to the preparatory position, the head remains turned to the left. On &, the position is held; assemblé soutenu is then executed with the other leg.

Assemblé soutenu, like the assemblé jump, is also executed in the opposite direction. In this case the movement is begun with the leg which is in fifth position in front, and the head turns away from the working leg.

Having mastered assemblé soutenu, it is executed in the small poses.

Example Initial position: as described above.

The right leg is stretched in second position, the arms are opened to the side, the head turns to the left. When the legs are joined together in fifth position on point, with the left leg in front, the left arm is closed in first position; the right one remains open in second and the head remains turned to the left.

In assemblé soutenu in the opposite direction, the left leg is opened from fifth position in front, to second position; the arms are opened to the side and the head turns to the right. When the legs are joined together in fifth position on point, with the right leg in front, the right arm is closed in first position; the left one remains opened in second position and the head remains turned.

Remarks In assemblé soutenu the torso is 'pulled up' and easy, particularly when the legs are drawn together in fifth position on point. The leg slides to the side, exactly along a straight line, and returns to fifth position on point along the same track, sustaining the turnout.

The character of the musical accompaniment combines the flow of the demi plié with short, brisk soutenu. The time signature is 2/4; assemblé soutenu is executed in one bar. Later on, the movement begins on the upbeat: on 2, demi plié; on &, the leg slides to the side; on 1, relevé on point in fifth position.

Pas glissade on point

At first pas glissade is studied to the side: from point 7 to point 3 of the class diagram, with the right leg, and from point 3 to point 7 of the class diagram with the left one.

Pas glissade on point to the side Initial position: fifth position en face, right leg in front, arms in the preparatory position, the head is turned to the right.

On 1 &, demi plié in fifth position, the arms opening on the upbeat, are raised through the preparatory position into first; the head inclines to the left, the eyes are directed towards the hands. On 2 &, the right leg is stretched with a sliding movement in the direction of point 3 of the class diagram, the left arm is opened in second position, the right one remains in first and the head turns to the right. On 3 &, the right leg rises on point, on the spot indicated by the pointed toe, and the left leg is drawn immediately towards the right one in fifth position behind; the body weight is centralised over both legs at the conclusion of pas glissade. On 4 &, fifth position on point is held, the arms and head remain in the assumed positions. On 1 of the following bar, demi plié in fifth position: pas glissade is repeated until the end of the musical phrase. At the conclusion of the last glissade, both arms are lowered in preparatory position.

Having mastered pas glissade to the side starting with the front foot, it is studied travelling in the same direction, starting with the back foot. Initial position: fifth position en face, right leg behind, the head is turned to the left.

On 1 &, demi plié in fifth position. The arms, opening on the upbeat, are raised through the preparatory position into first, the head inclines slightly, the eyes are directed towards the hands. On 2 &, the right leg is stretched with a sliding movement in the direction of point 3 of the class diagram, the left one remains in demi plié. The right arm is opened in second position, the left one remains in first position and the head turns to the left. On 3 &, the right leg rises on point on the spot indicated by the pointed toe and the left one is drawn immediately towards the right one, in fifth position in front. On 4 &, fifth position on point is held, the arms and head remain in the assumed positions. On 1 & of the following bar, demi plié in fifth position: glissade is continued until the end of the musical phrase. At the conclusion of the last glissade, both arms are lowered in preparatory position.

Later on, pas glissade, travelling in one direction to the side, is executed with a change of the legs, also changing the position of the arms and the turn of the head with each glissade.

Example Initial position: fifth position en face, right leg in front, arms in the preparatory position, the head turned to the right.

On the upbeat the arms, opening, are raised in first position. On 1, simultaneously with demi plié in fifth position, the left arm is opened in second position, the right one remains in first, the head turns to the right. On 2 &, the right leg is opened to the side, the head remains turned to the right. On 3 &, the right leg rises on point, the left one is drawn up to fifth position in front; the left arm, lowering slightly, is closed in first position and the head turns to the left. On 4 &, fifth position on point, the positions of arms and head are held. On 1 &, demi plié: the positions of arms and head remain the same. On 2 &, the right leg is opened to the side, the left arm is opened in second position, the head remains turned to the left. On 3 &, the right leg rises on point, the left one is drawn up to fifth position behind; the right arm, lowering slightly, is closed in first position, the head turns to the right and the left arm remains in second position. On 4 &, fifth position on point, the positions of arms and head are held.

Later on, pas glissade travelling to the side is also studied on the diagonal, from point 6 to point 2 of the class diagram with the right leg, and from point 4 to point 8 with the left one.

Remarks Pas glissade on point is at first studied facing the barre; the arms, maintaining their position opposite the centre of the torso, slide along the barre during the movement; the body weight is centred evenly over both legs.

Having mastered pas glissade to the side, it is studied in the poses croisée and effacée.

Pas glissade croisée en avant Initial position: fifth position épaulement croisé, right foot in front.

On 1 &, demi plié in fifth position; the arms, opening on the upbeat, return to the preparatory position. On 2 &, the right leg is stretched croisé devant with a sliding movement, the arms are raised in first position, the head inclines to the left, the eyes are directed towards the hands. On 3 &, the right leg rises on point on the spot indicated by the pointed toe, the left leg is drawn up towards the right one, in

fig. 55   Pas glissade croisée en avant

fifth position on point; the right arm is opened in second position, the left one remains in first and the head turns to the right. On 4 &, fifth position on point is held. On 1 & of the following bar, demi plié in fifth position and pas glissade croisé en avant is repeated until the end of the musical phrase; the arms and head remain in the assumed positions. At the conclusion of the last pas glissade, the arms are lowered in preparatory position (fig. 55).

Pas glissade croisé en arrière Initial position: fifth position épaulement croisé, right foot in front.

On 1 &, demi plié in fifth position; the arms, opening on the upbeat, return to the preparatory position. On 2 &, the left leg is stretched into croisée derrière with a sliding movement; the arms are raised in first position, the head inclines to the left and the eyes are directed towards the hands. On 3 &, the left leg rises

143

on point on the spot indicated by the pointed toe, the right one is drawn up towards the left one, in fifth position on point. The right arm is opened in second position, the left one remains in first and the head turns to the right. On 4 &, fifth position on point is held. On 1 & of the following bar, demi plié in fifth position: pas glissade croisé en arrière is continued until the end of the musical phrase; the arms and head remain in the assumed positions. At the conclusion of the last glissade, the arms are lowered in preparatory position.

Pas glissade effacé en avant and en arrière are executed according to the same rules, keeping in mind the character of these poses.

Remarks Later on, pas glissade in croisée are executed with the arms in the small and in the big poses. In the pose effacée the basic positions are held. In pose croisée, beside the basic ones, other positions of the arms are allowed. In pas glissade en avant in the small and in the big pose croisée with the right leg, the left arm may be opened in second position and the right one in first in the small pose, or in third in the big pose, the head remaining turned to the right. Accordingly the torso in the small pose as well as in the big one is projected slightly forward, imparting a different character to the pose.

Having mastered pas glissade on point in all directions and poses, it is begun on the upbeat on two 1/8. For example: on the first 1/8, demi plié; on the second 1/8, the leg is stretched; on 1 follows pas glissade on point; on &, the position is held; on 2, demi plié in fifth position etc.

The time signature is 4/4 or 2/4. The character of the music is precise and lively.

Temps lié en avant on point
Initial position: fifth position épaulement croisé, right leg in front.

On 1 &, demi plié in fifth position. The arms, opening on the upbeat, are closed in preparatory position. On 2 &, the right leg is stretched in croisée devant with a sliding movement, the arms are raised in first position, the head inclines to the left, the eyes are directed towards the hands. On 3 &, increasing the 'pull up' of the torso, the right leg rises on point on the spot indicated by the pointed toe, the left leg is drawn immediately up towards the right one, in fifth position on point; the left arm is raised in third position, the right one is opened in second and the head turns to the right. On 4 &, the position is held. On 1 & of the following bar, with a turn en face, demi plié in fifth position, the left arm is lowered in first position, the right one remains in second position, the head turns en face, the eyes are directed towards the left hand. On 2 &, the right leg is stretched to the side in the direction of point 3 of the class diagram, the left one remains in demi plié, the left arm is opened in second position and the head turns to the left. On 3 &, the 'pull up' of the torso is increased as the right leg transfers to point, on the spot indicated by the pointed toe; the left leg is drawn immediately towards the right one, in fifth position in front, épaulement croisé, the arms and head remain in the assumed positions. On 4 &, the position is held. On 1 & of the following bar, demi plié in fifth position, the arms are lowered in preparatory position and temps lié en avant is repeated with the other leg.

Temps lié en arrière on point

Initial position: as described above.

On 1 &, demi plié in fifth position; the arms, opening on the upbeat, are closed in preparatory position. On 2 &, the left leg is stretched in croisée derrière with a sliding mvement, the arms are raised in first position, the head inclines to the left, the eyes are directed towards the hands. On 3 &, the 'pull up' of the torso is increased as the left leg transfers to point, on the spot indicated by the pointed toe; the right leg is drawn up into fifth position on point, the left arm is raised in third position, the right one is opened in second and the head turns to the right. On 4 &, the position is held. On 1 & of the following bar, with a turn en face, demi plié in fifth position, the left arm is lowered in first position, the right one remains in second, the head turns en face and the eyes are directed towards the left hand. On 2 &, the left leg is stretched to the side in the direction of point 7 of the class diagram, the right leg remains in demi plié; the left arm is opened in second position and the head turns to the left. On 3 &, the 'pull up' of the torso is increased as the left leg transfers onto point, on the spot indicated by the pointed toe; the right leg is drawn immediately towards the left one, in fifth position behind, épaulement croisé, the arms and head remaining in the assumed positions. On 4 &, the position is held. On 1 & of the following bar, demi plié in fifth position, the arms are lowered in preparatory position and temps lié en arrière is repeated with the other leg.

Remarks In temps lié on point, the flow and smoothness of the movement are indispensable, particularly when lowering into demi plié from fifth position on point; the rules for glissade must also be observed, as this is a component part of temps lié on point.

Pas suivi

At first, pas suivi is executed on the spot. When the legs have acquired a sufficient degree of precision it is executed travelling along a straight line, from point 7 towards point 3 of the class diagram with the right leg, and from point 3 towards point 7 with the left one. Later on, pas suivi is executed on the diagonal, from point 6 towards point 2 of the class diagram with the right leg, and from point 4 towards point 8 with the left one.

Pas suivi along a straight line Initial position: fifth position en face, right leg in front, arms in the preparatory position, the head is turned to the right. Two introductory chords; préparation. On the first chord, demi plié in fifth position; the arms, opening slightly on the upbeat, are raised through the preparatory position into first, the head inclines to the left, the eyes are directed towards the hands. On the second chord, relevé on point in fifth position; the left arm is opened in second position, the right one is raised in third, the head, turning to the right, inclines slightly, the eyes are directed past the elbow of the right arm. On &, the pointed toe of the right leg is raised slightly off the floor; on 1, it is placed on the floor, travelling sideways; on &, the toe of the left leg is raised off the floor and, as if catching up with the right leg, it is placed behind it in fifth position.

Alternately raising the toe of each leg off the floor with an almost imperceptible bend of the knee, one should travel in the direction of point 3 of the class diagram for eight bars of 4/4. During this, the torso should remain 'pulled up' and completely calm, the arms and head remaining in the assumed positions.

At the conclusion of the exercise, two concluding chords: on the first, the right arm is opened in second position, the head turns to the right, fifth position on point is held; on the second chord, demi plié in fifth position, the arms are lowered into preparatory position.

Pas suivi on the diagonal follows the same rules.

Remarks In fifth position the legs, particularly the back one, are turned out; the 'pulled up' and calm torso enables one to travel lightly on point. The shoulders are level and lowered, the arms remain in the correct positions, the neck remains free while the head is turned to the right.

Pas suivi en tournant At first, pas suivi en tournant is executed separately; later on, it is combined with pas suivi along a straight line or on the diagonal, or with other movements on point.

Initial position: fifth position, épaulement croisé, right leg in front.

On two introductory chords, relevé on point in fifth position; the arms are opened through first position, the right one into third position, the left one into second. Now follows a turn of 360° to the right on the spot, around one's own axis, according to the rules for pas suivi. At first, the head turns to the left, returning without delay to the right. The fifth position on point is turned out, the torso is 'pulled up'.

On two concluding chords, the right arm is opened in second position and both arms are lowered into preparatory position, simultaneously with demi plié in fifth position.

Remarks At first, the turn should be executed not faster than in one bar of 4/4. Each 1/4 should coincide with a quarter turn, which ensures the evenness of the turn. Later on, pas suivi is executed in a faster tempo: two turns to a bar of 4/4. The arms may assume different positions, but the rules of execution of the turn are adhered to.

The time signature is 4/4, 3/4 or 2/4. The character of the music is light, precise and lively.

Sissonne simple on point

Initial position: fifth position en face, right leg in front, arms in the preparatory position, head turned to the right.

On 1 &, demi plié in fifth position. On 2, the left leg, pushing away from the floor, rises on point, the right leg, increasing the turnout, is raised energetically to the conditional cou-de-pied position; the head turns to the left, the arms remain in the preparatory position. On 3, the right leg, sustaining the turnout, is lowered into the fifth position, through the cou-de-pied derrière; sissonne simple is concluded in fifth position in demi plié, with the left leg in front and the head turned to the left. On 4, the legs are straightened and sissonne simple is then executed with the other leg (fig. 56).

fig. 56
Sissonne
simple devant

fig. 57
Sissonne
simple derrière

Sissonne simple in the opposite direction On 1, demi plié in fifth position. On 2, the right leg, pushing away from the floor, rises on point; the left leg is raised energetically sur le cou-de-pied derrière, the head turns to the left, the arms remain in the preparatory position. On 3, the left leg, increasing the turnout of the heel, comes down through the conditional cou-de-pied position into fifth position in front; sissonne simple is concluded in demi plié in fifth position, left leg in front, with the head turned to the left. On 4, the legs are straightened and sissonne simple is then executed with the other leg (fig. 57).

Later on, sissonne simple may be varied, executing it several times on one and the same leg. For example: twice sissonne simple without changing fifth position, the third time changing fifth position. On 4, a pause. The same thing can be executed in the opposite direction. After it has been mastered, sissonne simple is begun on the upbeat. On 2 &, demi plié: on 1 & sissonne simple; on 2 &, demi plié in fifth position, etc. Later still, sissonne simple is executed in épaulement, and arm movements are then included.

Example 1 Initial position: fifth position, épaulement croisé, right leg in front.

The anacrusis is divided into two 1/8. On the first 1/8, the arms are opened; on the second 1/8, demi plié, the arms are raised through the preparatory position into first, the head inclines to the left, the eyes are directed towards the hands. On 1, a turn towards point 2 of the class diagram; the left leg executes relevé on point, the right one, increasing the turnout, is raised to the conditional cou-de-pied position. The left arm is opened in second position, the right one remains in first, both hands are opened, the head inclines slightly to the left and the eyes are directed towards the right hand. On 2, the right leg is lowered through cou-de-pied derrière into fifth position demi plié, left foot in front, the arms and head remaining in the assumed positions. On 1, sissonne simple with the left leg, turning towards point 8 of the class diagram; the left arm goes through the raised preparatory position to first position, the right one to second position; both hands are opened, the head inclines slightly to the right and the eyes are directed towards the left hand On 2, demi plié etc.

Example 2 Initial position: fifth position, épaulement croisé left leg in front, the head turned to the left.

The anacrusis is divided into two 1/8. On the first 1/8, the arms are opened; on the second 1/8, demi plié, the arms are raised through the preparatory position into first, the head inclines to the right and the eyes are directed towards the hands. On 1, with a turn towards point 8 of the class diagram, the left leg executes relevé on point; the right one, increasing the turnout, is raised to the conditional cou-de-pied position; the right arm is opened in second position, the left one remains in first, the hands are opened, the head turns towards point 8 of the class diagram and the eyes are directed towards the left hand, On 2, demi plié in fifth position, right leg in front. On 1, sissonne simple with the left leg, turning towards point 2 of the class diagram; the right arm passes through the raised preparatory position into first, the left one is opened in second position, the hands are opened, the head turns towards point 2 of the class diagram and the eyes are directed towards the right hand. On 2, demi plié in fifth position etc.

After the basic form of sissonne simple has been mastered, it is also executed using other positions of the arms and head. The arm movements are free and supple.

Remarks In sissonne simple, the supporting leg is taut and turned out, the working leg is turned out and energetic and the torso is 'pulled up'. The turns of the torso and head, and the co-ordination of the arms should be very precise. The arm movements are free.

The character of the musical accompaniment is precise and energetic.

The Third Year of Study

The exercises of the third class

In the third year the mastering of the alphabet of the classical dance is consolidated; this is the necessary foundation on which the movements of the classical dance can be built and developed. This is why here, as well as in the first two years, correctness and clarity of execution must be produced before anything else. Strength and endurance must be developed. Stability must be consolidated in exercises on demi-point in the centre of the room.

At the same time, the development of future artistry, using elements of artistic colouring of movements (as already mentioned in several exercises from the preceding years) is now begun. On the other hand, in order to achieve this, one should not over-complicate the combinations.

The new movements from the syllabus of the third year are at first studied in their purest form. In comparison with the second year, the musical accompaniment of the lesson now demands more variation in rhythmical structure and a general acceleration in tempo.

Exercices à la barre

The exercises at the barre repeat and develop those of the second year. A device is introduced to test the balance on the supporting leg. At the conclusion of some of the exercises, the balance is held on demi-point on the supporting leg, taking the hands off the barre. During this the working leg may be sur le cou-de-pied devant or derrière, or it may be extended in the air at 45° or at 90° in any given direction. This device allows one to test and correct oneself and to consolidate stability at the same time.

When executing battement frappé, battement double frappé and battement soutenu at 90°, épaulement croisé and effacé are gradually introduced.

In the second half of the year, exercises such as battement fondu with plié relevé, and with demi rond de jambe en dehors and en dedans, are executed in all directions and poses. The more difficult pose écartée is at first studied in battement tendu jeté, later on in grand battement jeté, and in battement relevé and développé.

All turns in épaulement demand a precise co-ordination of torso, legs, arms and head, corresponding with the character of the poses, which must be sustained throughout the execution of the exercise. When executing an exercise in épaulement, it is important to sustain the position of the supporting foot. In battement relevé lent at 90°, and in battement développé, a rise on demi-point is added. At first, these exercises are executed en face in all directions; later on, in the poses.

The 'pulled up' torso and the extreme tautness of the leg enable one to raise the heel off the floor with ease, sustaining its turnout. The rise on demi-point happens after the working leg has assumed the given direction or pose.

> *Example* Battement relevé or développé is executed on 2/4 of a bar; on the third 1/4, rise on demi-point. On the fourth 1/4, the position is held. On the first 1/4 of the following bar, the heel of the supporting leg is lowered to the floor without disturbing the position of the working leg. At the end of the bar, développé is concluded in fifth position.

In the second half of the year, demi ronds de jambe en l'air at 90°[1] en dehors and en dedans are added to the exercises on demi-point. In this exercise, it is necessary to sustain the tautness of the supporting leg on demi-point and the even positioning of the supporting foot on the floor.

Battement double fondu

Initial position: fifth position, right leg in front, right arm in the preparatory position, the head turned to the right.

On the upbeat, the right arm is opened slightly. On 1, demi plié with the supporting leg; the working leg is raised to the conditional cou-de-pied position, the right arm returns to the preparatory position, the head inclines slightly to the left. On &, the supporting leg, gradually straightening the knee, is raised to

---

[1] *See* rules of execution for rond de jambe en l'air at 90° in the second year.

three-quarter point; the working leg maintains a turned out cou-de-pied position. The right arm is raised in first position, the head inclines to the left, the eyes are directed towards the hand. On 2, the supporting leg, lowering the heel to the floor, transfers to demi plié; the working leg is stretched to the side at 45° (the turnout of both legs is increased), the right arm is opened in second position and the head turns to the right. On &, the supporting leg, gradually straightening the knee, is raised to three-quarter point, the working leg remains at 45° and is turned out, the arms and head remain in the assumed positions. On 1 of the following bar, the supporting leg, lowering the heel to the floor, transfers to demi plié, the working leg is bent sur le cou-de-pied derrière; the right arm is lowered in preparatory position, the head, while turned to the right, is lowered slightly, with the eyes directed towards the hand. On &, the supporting leg, gradually straightening, is raised to three-quarter point; the working leg maintains a turned out cou-de-pied derrière positon, the right arm is raised in first position,the head inclines to the left and the eyes are directed towards the hand. On 2, the supporting leg, lowering the heel to the floor, transfers to demi plié; the working leg is stretched to the side at 45°, the right arm is opened in second position, the head turns to the right. On &, the supporting leg, gradually straightening the knee, is raised to three-quarter point; the working leg remains turned out at 45°, the arms and head remain in the assumed positions.

Having mastered battement double fondu to the side, it is executed according to the same rules to the front and to the back. Later on, battement double fondu is executed with demi rond de jambe at 45°, in all directions, en dehors and en dedans.

Example In battement double fondu, the working leg is stretched to the front at 45°, the supporting leg executes demi plié. Then, gradually straightening, the supporting leg is raised to three-quarter point, at the same time the working leg, remaining at 45°, is brought to second position, etc.

Remarks In battement double fondu the torso is 'pulled up', the legs are extremely turned out, the hand rests easily upon the barre, remaining in one and the same place.

The time signature and the character of the music are the same as for battement fondu (see the first year).

153

Battement soutenu at 90°

Initial position: fifth position, right leg in front.

The anacrusis is divided into three 1/8. On the first 1/8, the right arm is opened slightly; on the second 1/8, it is closed into the preparatory position simultaneously with a rise in fifth position on demi-point; on the third 1/8, the position is held. On 1, the working leg is raised, through the conditional cou-de-pied position to the middle of the knee, the arm is raised in first position, the head inclines to the left, as the 'pull up' of the torso is increased. On 2, the working leg, increasing the turnout, is extended to the front at 90°, according to the rules for battement développé. Simultaneously, the supporting leg, lowering the heel to the floor, begins demi plié; the arm is opened in second position and the head turns to the right. On &, the supporting leg continues demi plié as the working leg is raised still higher. On 3, the working leg is gradually lowered and, touching the floor with pointed toes, it is immediately drawn forwards to fifth position, at the same time as the supporting leg is gradually straightened. On 4, both legs are stretched simultaneously in fifth position on demi-point, the torso remains 'pulled up' and the right arm is lowered into the preparatory position. '&' is the upbeat for the following battement soutenu. Battement soutenu is executed in all directions. When battement soutenu is repeated in one and the same direction, the arm remains in second position. When changing to another direction, the arm is opened again in second position through the preparatory and first positions. Having mastered battement soutenu in all directions, en face, at the barre, and in the centre, it is executed in the big poses croisée and effacée (fig. 58).

fig. 58   Battement soutenu at 90°

Example Battement soutenu in the pose croisée devant in the centre. Initial position: fifth position, épaulement croisé, right foot in front.

The anacrusis is divided into three 1/8. On the first 1/8, the arms are opened slightly; on the second 1/8, they are closed in preparatory position simultaneously with a rise in fifth position on demi-point. On the third 1/8, the position is held. On 1 &, the working leg is raised through the conditional cou-de-pied position to the middle of the knee of the supporting leg; the arms are raised in first position, the head inclines to the left, the 'pull up' of the torso is increased. On 2, the working leg is extended to the front, according to the rules for développé; simultaneously, the supporting leg, lowering the heel to the floor, begins demi plié. The left arm is raised in third position, the right one is opened in second, the head turns to the right. On &, the supporting leg continues demi plié, the working leg is raised still higher. On 3, the working leg begins to lower. The left arm is opened in second position, continuing the movement; the working leg, touching the floor with pointed toes, is immediately drawn towards fifth position as the supporting leg is gradually straightened. On 4, both legs are stretched simultaneously in fifth position, on demi-point, the arms are lowered into preparatory position and the head is turned to the right, the torso remaining 'pulled up'. '&' is the upbeat for the following battement soutenu. Battement soutenu in croisée derrière and in the poses effacée devant and derrière is executed according to the same rules, observing the character of the given poses.

Remarks In battement soutenu, the supporting leg, coming down from demi-point, remains turned out and begins demi plié only after the heel touches the floor. In all directions, the legs are extremely turned out and must be drawn into fifth position absolutely simultaneously. The torso is 'pulled up' at all times, the movements of the arms are free and supple.

The character of the musical accompaniment is smooth and flowing. At first, battement soutenu is executed in one bar of 4/4. Later on, in one bar of 2/4.

Example The anacrusis is divided into three 1/8. On the first 1/8, the arms are opened; on the second 1/8, they are closed in preparatory position simultaneously with a rise on demi-point; on the third 1/8, the working leg is raised through the conditional cou-de-pied position to the middle of the knee, the arms are raised in first position, the head inclines to the left. On 1, the working leg is extended at 90°, etc.

Détourné

Détourné towards the barre Initial position: fifth position, right leg in front. The left hand rests easily upon the barre, the right arm is opened in second position, the head is turned to the right.

On the upbeat, demi plié in fifth position on three-quarter point, the 'pull up' of the torso is increased, the arms are brought together in first position through the raised preparatory position and the head turns en face. On 2, a turn of 360° is executed in the direction of the barre: the taut legs, preserving the turnout of the heels, are changed so that at the end of the turn the left leg is located in front; first position of the arms is maintained during the turn and the head turns to the right at the beginning of the turn; as quickly as possible, as if catching up with the turn, it assumes the en face position. On 3, the left hand is placed lightly upon the barre, the right arm is opened in second position and the head turns to the right. 4 is the upbeat for détourné away from the barre.

Détourné away from the barre Initial position: fifth position, right leg behind. The left hand rests upon the barre, the right arm is opened in second position, the head is turned to the right.

On the upbeat, demi plié in fifth position. On 1, the legs execute relevé in fifth position on three-quarter point, the 'pull up' of the torso is increased, the arms are brought together in first position through the raised preparatory position and the head turns en face. On 2, a turn of 360° is executed, away from the barre: the taut legs, increasing the turnout of the heels, are changed so that at the end of the turn the right leg is located in front; the first position of the arms is maintained during the turn, the head turns to the left at the beginning of the turn and as quickly as possible, as if catching up with the turn, it assumes the en face position. On 3, the left hand is placed lightly upon the barre, the right arm is opened in second position, the head turns to the right. 4 is the upbeat for détourné towards the barre.

Remarks The turn of the torso must coincide exactly with the turn of the legs: the precise co-ordination of the arms and the turn of the head stimulate the turn. Later on, détourné is introduced in any given exercise at the barre, as well as in the centre. It can be executed in the middle of the exercise or at the end.

The musical accompaniment for détourné depends on the exercise with which it is combined.

Grand rond de jambe en dehors at 90°
Initial position: fifth position, right leg in front.

On &, the right arm is opened on the upbeat. On 1 &, it is raised through the preparatory position into first position. The head inclines to the left, the working leg is raised through the conditional cou-de-pied position to the middle of the knee of the supporting leg. On 2 &, the working leg is extended to the front at 90°, the arms and head remaining in the assumed positions. On 3 & 4 &, the working leg is raised as it is drawn to the side, the arm is opened in second position, the head turns to the right. On 1 & 2 & of the second bar, the working leg continues to be raised as it is carried to the back; the torso, resisting the unavoidable inclination, is projected slightly forward. On 3 &, the position is held. On 4 &, the working leg is closed in fifth position behind, the torso is brought upright and the arm is lowered into the preparatory position.

Grand rond de jambe en dedans at 90°
Initial position: fifth position, right leg behind.

On 1 &, the right arm is opened on the upbeat. On 1 &, it is raised, through the preparatory position, into first position; the head inclines slightly to the left, the working leg is raised through the cou-de-pied derrière to the knee of the supporting leg. On 2 &, the working leg is extended to the back, the torso, resisting the unavoidable inclination, is projected slightly forward; the arms and head remain in the assumed positions. On 3 & 4 &, the working leg is raised as it is drawn to the side; the torso having been brought upright, and the 'pull up' increased, the arm is opened into second position, the head turns to the right, with the eyes following the hand. On 1 & 2 & of the second bar, the working leg, continuing to be raised, is carried to the front. On 3 &, the position is held. On 4 &, the working leg is closed into fifth position in front and the arm is lowered into the preparatory position.

Remarks In grand rond de jambe at 90°, the weight of the body is centred exactly over the extremely taut supporting leg. As the working leg describes an arc, both legs must be taut and turned out. The hips are absolutely level. It is necessary to maintain the correct position of the arms carefully, as they tend to react to the movement of the working leg.

After mastering grand ronds de jambe at 90° en dehors and en dedans, they are executed in the centre. Both arms are raised in first position simultaneously with the développé to the front or to the back. At the beginning of the rond de jambe en dehors or en dedans, they are opened in second position, remaining there until the end of the movement.

The time signature is 4/4. the character of the music is legato. At first, grand rond de jambe is executed in two bars of 4/4: once this has been mastered, in one bar. In this case, on &, the leg is raised to the level of the knee; on 1, it is stretched forward, etc. Later on, 3/4 and 6/8 time may be utilised.

Pas coupé

Pas coupé is an auxiliary movement in classical dance and that is why it is always executed combined with other movements. It is used in the exercises at the barre and in the centre, but also in jumps and point exercises. The name of pas coupé – 'cutting' – defines its short, sharp character: in any given combination, pas coupé is always executed on 1/8.

Example Initial position: fifth position, right leg behind, the left hand rests upon the barre.

On two introductory chords, the right leg is opened to the side at 45°; at the same time, the left leg rises on demi-point, the right arm is opened in second position and the head turns to the right. On 1 &, the right leg comes down in demi plié in front of the left leg, taking its place;

the left leg is immediately raised sur le cou-de-pied derrière, the right arm is lowered into the raised preparatory position and the head is turned to the right and slightly lowered. On 2, the left leg quickly steps onto three-quarter point, replacing the right one, which is opened immediately to the side at 45°, via the conditional cou-de-pied position. The right arm is opened through first into second position and the head turns to the right. On &, the position is held. On 1 & of the second bar, the right leg comes down in demi plié behind the left one, taking its place; the left leg is immediately raised to the conditional cou-de-pied position. The positions of the head and of the right arm are maintained. On 2, the left leg steps quickly onto three-quarter point replacing the right one, which is immediately opened to the side, at 45°, via cou-de-pied derrière. The positions of the head and of the right arm are maintained. On &, the position is held.

Remarks Pas coupé is concluded in an open position, at 45° or sur le cou-de-pied, depending on the given exercise.

Example Pas coupé at the barre, combined with battement fondu and battement frappé. The exercise is executed in eight bars. The time signature is 4/4.

Initial position: fifth position, right foot in front.

On two 1/4 of the first bar, battement fondu to the front; on the following two 1/4, plié relevé with rond de jambe en dehors at 45°. On two 1/4 of the second bar, battement fondu to the side; on the third 1/4, tombé with the right leg in front of the left one, which is raised sur le cou-de-pied derrière. The right arm is brought to the raised preparatory position, the head is turned to the right and slightly lowered. On the first half of the fourth 1/4, coupé; the left leg steps onto three-quarter point, replacing the right one, which is opened through the conditional cou-de-pied position to the side, at 45°. The right arm is opened through first position into second and the head turns to the right. On the second half of the fourth 1/4, the position is held. On two 1/4 of the third bar, battement fondu to the back; on two 1/4 plié relevé with rond de jambe en dedans at 45°. On two 1/4 of the fourth bar, battement fondu to the side.

On the third 1/4, tombé on the right leg behind the left one, which is raised to the conditional cou-de-pied position. The right arm remains in second position and the head turns to the right. On the first half of the fourth 1/4, coupé; the left leg steps onto three-quarter point, the right one is opened, through the cou-de-pied derrière, to the side at 45°. The arm and head remain in the assumed positions. On the second half of the fourth 1/4, the position is held. On the fifth bar, execute four battements frappés: two to the front and two to the side, each on 1/4. On three 1/4 of the sixth bar, three doubles frappés to the side. On the first half of the fourth 1/4, tombé on the right leg in front of the left one, which is raised sur le cou-de-pied derrière; the right arm is brought to the raised preparatory position, the head is turned to the right and lowered. On the second half of the fourth 1/4, coupé; the left leg steps onto three-quarter point, replacing the right one, which is opened through the conditional cou-de-pied to the side, at 45°. The right arm is opened through first position into second position and the head turns to the right. On the seventh bar, four battements frappés, two to the back and two to the side. On three 1/4 of the eighth bar, three doubles frappés to the side; on the first half of the fourth 1/4, tombé on the right leg, behind the left one, which is raised in the conditional cou-de-pied position; the right arm remains in second position, the head turns to the right. On the second half of the fourth 1/4, coupé; the left leg steps onto three-quarter point, the right one is opened through the cou-de-pied derrière, into second position at 45°, the right arm and the head remain in the assumed positions. On two concluding chords, the exercise is ended in fifth position.

Remarks The above example is not the only possible one: pas coupé may be executed in any given exercise.

Half turn en dehors and en dedans changing the legs
These half turns are studied at the barre and, depending on the exercise, they are executed on the whole foot or on the demi-point.

Half turn en dehors Initial position: fifth position, right leg behind.

On two introductory chords, the right leg is opened in second position with the toes on the floor; the right arm is opened in second position and the head turns to the right. On 1, the right leg is closed in fifth position in front and, without delay, a turn of 180° is executed on the same leg, towards the barre, that is to say en dehors, to the left. During the turn, the left leg is opened to the side, passing through the conditional cou-de-pied position; it finishes at the conclusion of the turn in second position, with the toes on the floor. The right arm, which was sent to first position at the beginning of the turn, is placed upon the barre at its conclusion. The left arm is opened through first position, into second. The head is turned to the left at the end of the turn.

Half turn en dedans Initial position: fifth position, right leg in front.

On two introductory chords, the right leg is opened in second position with the toes on the floor; the right arm is opened in second position, the head turns to the right. On 1, the right leg is closed into fifth position behind and, without delay, on the same leg a turn of 180° is executed away from the barre, that is to say, en dedans, to the right. During the turn, the left leg is opened to the side, passing through the cou-de-pied derrière; it finishes at the conclusion of the turn in second position, with the toes on the floor. The left arm, which had been sent to first position at the beginning of the turn, is opened in second position. The right hand is placed upon the barre at the end of the turn. The head turns to the left.

Remarks During the turn on the whole foot, the heel is slightly raised. The turn must be executed on one foot only, therefore at the beginning, the other foot is raised immediately sur le cou-de-pied. It is particularly important to observe this rule when executing the turn en dedans away from the barre. The arms are taken off the barre at the beginning of the turn in order not to hamper the movement.

These half turns are executed after battement tendu. If a half turn is executed after tendu jeté the working leg will be opened at 25° before and after the turn, corresponding to the movement with which it is combined.

When combined with battement fondu, battement frappé, battement double frappé, rond de jambe en l'air and petit battement sur le cou-de-pied executed on demi-point, the turns are executed on three-quarter point. The rules of execution are the same except that the working leg is opened at 45° before and after the turns. Sometimes the turns are executed at the beginning of an exercise, but more often in the middle or at the end.

The time signature depends on the exercise with which the half turns are combined.

Tombé with half turn sur le cou-de-pied en dehors and en dedans

Half turn en dehors Initial position: fifth position, right leg behind.

On two introductory chords, the right leg is opened to the side at 45°, the right arm is opened, through first position, into second and the head turns to the right.

On 1, tombé with the right leg in front of the left one, which is raised immediately sur le cou-de-pied derrière. The right arm is brought to the raised preparatory position, the head is turned to the right and slightly lowered. On 2, a turn of 180° en dehors is executed on the right leg to the left (towards the barre). At the beginning of the turn, the right leg is raised to three-quarter point, forcefully stretching the knee; the left leg, increasing the turnout, is brought to the front, to conditional cou-de-pied; the torso and hips are completely 'pulled up'. At the beginning of the half turn, the right arm is raised in first position and the head turns to the right; at the conclusion of the half turn, the right hand is placed upon the barre, the left arm is opened, through first position, into second and the head turns to the left.

Half turn en dedans Initial position: fifth position, right leg in front.

On two introductory chords, the right leg is opened in second position at 45°, the right arm is opened in second position and the head turns to the right.

On 1, tombé with the right leg behind the left one, which is raised immediately to the conditional cou-de-pied; the right arm and the position of the head are maintained. On 2, a turn of 180° en dedans is executed on the right leg to the right (away from the barre). At the beginning of the turn, the right leg is raised to three-quarter point, forcefully stretching the knee, the left leg, increasing the turnout, is brought sur le cou-de-pied derrière with the torso and hips completely 'pulled up'. At the beginning of the turn, the left hand is taken off the barre and sent to first position, opening into second at the conclusion of the turn. The right hand is placed upon the barre at the end of the half turn and the head turns to the left.

Remarks During the execution of the half turn, the legs must be turned out, the supporting leg taut. The hand is taken off the barre at the beginning of the turn in order not to hamper it.

The time signature depends on the exercise with which the turns are combined.

Preparatory exercise for tours from fifth position en dehors and en dedans

Tours and preparatory exercises for tours are at first studied in the centre, and only after mastering the correct devices are they used in exercises at the barre, as tours executed at the barre are more difficult than tours executed in the centre.

At the barre we first study preparatory exercises for tours.

Preparatory exercise for tour en dehors Initial position: fifth position, right leg in front. The left hand is resting upon the barre, the right arm is in the preparatory position, the head is turned to the right.

On 1 &, demi plié in fifth position; the right arm, opening slightly on the upbeat, is raised through the preparatory position into first position, the head turns en face, the eyes are directed to the front. On 2 &, with a push of the heel away from the floor, the left leg executes a relevé on three-quarter point and the right one is raised to the conditional cou-de-pied position; the left arm is united with the right one in first position, the head remains en face. On 3 & 4, the position is held. On 1 & 2 of the following bar, the right leg increases the turnout as it comes down into demi plié in fifth position behind. The right arm is opened in second position, the left hand returns to the barre and the head turns to the right. On 3 & 4, initial position.

Preparatory exercise for tour en dedans Initial position; fifth position, right leg behind, the left hand is resting upon the barre, the right arm is in the preparatory position with the head turned to the right.

On 1 &, demi plié in fifth position, the right arm, opening slightly on the upbeat, is carried through the preparatory and first positions into second. The head turns en face, the eyes are directed to the front. On 2 &, with a push of the heel away from the floor, the left leg executes relevé on three-quarter point; the right one, increasing the turnout of the thigh and of the heel, is raised to the conditional cou-de-pied; the left arm is united with the right one in first position and the head remains en face. On 3 & 4 &, the position is held. On 1 & 2 & of the following bar, the right leg, sustaining the turnout of the thigh, comes down in demi plié in fifth position in front; the right arm is opened in second position, the left one returns to the barre. On 3 & 4 &, initial position.

Remarks For the tour to be executed correctly, the arm must be taken off the barre together with the turn of the torso, in no case pushing away from the barre. After the tour, it is necessary to test the exact position of the torso on the supporting leg, after which the hand is placed upon the barre.

In preparatory exercises and tours the torso is calm, the supporting leg is on three-quarter point, taut and turned out; the working leg, being raised sur le cou-de-pied, is turned out and active and the hand rests freely upon the barre before the tour.

Preparatory exercises and tours are introduced into any exercises at the barre, in the middle as well as at the end of the exercise.

The time signature depends on the exercise with which the tours are combined.

Exercices au milieu

In the third year, the majority of the exercises in the centre are executed on demi-point, preserving the same order of alternation and the same methodical approach as at the barre. At first, the exercises are executed en face; later they are gradually transferred to épaulement, alternating both positions.

An indispensable condition for exercises on demi-point in the centre is stability in exercises on the whole foot.

Battement relevé lent at 90° and battement développé in all directions with a rise on demi-point are executed in the centre, having first mastered them at the barre. The poses of the classical dance with a rise on demi-point are not studied before the second half year.

> *Examples* On two 1/4 of the first bar, pose croisée devant; on the third 1/4, rise on demi-point; on the fourth 1/4, the position on demi-point is held. On two 1/4 of the second bar, the heel of the supporting leg is lowered to the floor, the arm is opened from third position into second; the position of the working leg is maintained. At the conclusion of the bar, both arms and the working leg are lowered into fifth position. Rises on demi-point in the other poses are executed according to the same rules.

Second and fourth arabesques, as well as the pose écartée, being the most difficult, are executed only on the whole foot. The rules of execution for grand rond de jambe en dehors and en dedans remain the same as at the barre. In développé to the front or to the back, both arms are raised in first position, opening into second position with the beginning of the rond de jambe, and remaining there until the end of the movement.

In adagio, in addition to the poses of the classical dance, the following movements are included: demi rond de jambe and grand rond de jambe en dehors and en dedans, détourné on demi-point, several ports de bras and pas de bourrées. It is necessary in adagio to obtain a logical succession of movements, avoiding excess of variety. The duration of the adagio must not exceed twelve or sixteen bars. The time signature is 4/4 or 6/8.

Having mastered pas coupé at the barre, it is executed in the centre and is also combined with several other movements.

> *Example* Pas coupé combined with rond de jambe en l'air and petits battements.
>
> The time signature is 4/4. The duration of the exercise is eight bars: four bars en dehors and four bars en dedans.

Initial position: fifth position, épaulement croisé, right leg in front.

On 1/4 of the first bar, temps relevé en dehors with a turn en face. On the following two 1/4, two ronds de jambe en l'air en dehors, each on a 1/4. On two 1/4 of the second bar, three ronds de jambe en l'air en dehors each on an 1/8. On the fourth 1/8, a pause at 45°. On the first half of the third 1/4, a turn to épaulement croisé, tombé with the right leg behind the left one, which is immediately raised to the conditional cou-de-pied; the right arm is closed into first position, the left arm remains in second and the head turns to the left. On the second half of the third 1/4, the position is held. On the first half of the last 1/4, coupé with a turn en face; the left leg steps onto three-quarter point, replacing the right one, which is immediately raised sur le cou-de-pied derrière; the right arm is opened into second position and the head turns en face. On the third bar, and on two 1/4 of the fourth, petits battements in 1/8s, accentuating the cou-de-pied devant. On the third 1/4, the right leg is opened in second position at 45°. On the fourth 1/4, it is closed in fifth position behind, épaulement croisé, and the arms are lowered into the preparatory position. For the following four bars, the exercise is repeated en dedans, beginning the temps relevé en dedans with the right leg.

Remarks The above example is not the only possible one; pas coupé may be combined with any kind of movement without losing its specific character.

Sixth port de bras
Initial position: fifth position épaulement croisé, right leg in front.

Two introductory chords: on 1, demi plié in fifth position; the arms, opening slightly on the upbeat, are returned to the preparatory position. On &, the right leg is stretched croisée devant, the arms are raised in first position, the head inclines slightly to the left. On 2, a transition onto the right leg according to the principles for temps lié; the left leg is extended to the back, the toe touching the floor. The right arm is opened in second position, the left one is raised in third and the head turns to the right (pose croisée derrière). On the upbeat, on &, the

166

head, turning en face, is raised, the eyes are directed towards the left hand and the arms, preserving their curve, are opened slightly, beginning at the fingertips, as if to lengthen the movement. On 1 & 2 &, with increased turnout of both legs, the supporting leg begins demi plié; gradually enlarging this, the taut right leg slides with the toe along the floor to croisé derrière, the 'pulled up' torso is projected forward, the arms and the head remaining in the assumed positions. On 3 &, the weight of the body is transferred over the left leg, which is placed on the floor on the spot indicated by the pointed toe. The right leg is drawn towards the left one in the pose croisée devant. The left arm is lowered and the right one is raised through the preparatory position and they are united in first position; the left shoulder is drawn slightly backwards, the head inclines to the left, with the eyes directed towards the hands. On 4 &, the right arm is raised in third position, the left one is opened in second and the head turns to the left. The 'pulled up' torso, keeping the hips level, bends backwards smoothly at the waist starting with the upper back. On 1 & 2 &, the backbend is continued, the right arm is opened in second position. On 3, the left arm is closed in third position, the head turns to the right. On & 4, the torso is brought upright gradually, returning to the initial position; the right leg, stepping forward, is placed upon the floor, the left one is stretched in the pose croisée derrière (fig. 59).

The movement is repeated, after which, on two concluding chords, the left arm is opened in second position and both arms are lowered in preparatory position and the left leg is closed in fifth position.

Remarks In sixth port de bras it is essential to achieve a smooth, flowing and absolutely uninterrupted execution and to observe an exact co-ordination of arms and head when the torso inclines forward and when it bends back; the arm movements are supple.

The time signature is 4/4 or 3/4. The character of the music is legato. At first, the port de bras is studied in two 4/4 bars or in eight 3/4 bars. Later on, the port de bras is executed in one 4/4 bar or in four 3/4 bars.

Preparatory exercise for tours

The preparatory exercises for tours are studied after having

fig. 59   Sixth port de bras

acquired a correct placement of the torso, turnout and tautness of the legs, and a developed instep, allowing one to maintain stability on three-quarter point.

Before the study of the preparatory exercises for tours, one should understand the concepts of turning en dehors and en dedans, with their preceding arm positions in the préparation.

A turn en dehors to the right is a turn to the right on the left leg. Before the turn, in préparation in any position, the left arm is opened in second position, the right one is in first position.

A turn en dedans to the right is a turn to the right on the right leg. Before the turn, in préparation in any position, the left arm is opened in second position, the right one is in first.

When turning to the left the positions of the arms are changed accordingly. The most correct way to cultivate the placement of the torso in tours is the preparatory exercise from second position.

Preparatory exercise for tours en dehors from second position
Initial position: fifth position épaulement croisé, right leg in front.

On the upbeat, demi plié in fifth position; the arms, opening slightly, return into the preparatory position. On 1 &, relevé on three-quarter point in fifth position with a turn en face; the arms are raised in first position, the head turns en face, the eyes are directed towards the front. On 2 &, fifth position on three-quarter point is held. On 3 &, the right leg is opened to the side at 45°, the arms are opened in second position. On 4, the position is held. On &, demi plié in second position; the right arm is closed in first position, the left one remains in second, the head and the focus remain en face. On 1 & of the second bar, the left leg, pushing away from the floor and maintaining the turnout of the heel, executes relevé on three-quarter point; the right one, increasing the turnout of the upper part and of the heel, is raised to the conditional cou-de-pied position. The arms are united in first position. On 2 &, the position on three-quarter point is held. On 3 &, the exercise is concluded in fifth position, épaulement croisé, in demi plié, left leg in front; the arms are opened, preserving their curve, the hands are opened forward and the head turns to the left. On 4 &, initial position.

Preparatory exercise for tours en dedans from second position
Initial position: fifth position, épaulement croisé, left leg in front.

On the upbeat, demi plié; the arms, opening slightly, return to the preparatory position. On 1 &, relevé on three-quarter point in fifth position, with a turn en face; the arms are raised in first position, the head turns en face, the eyes are directed to the front. On 2 &, fifth position on three-quarter point is held. On 3 &, the right leg is opened to the side at 45°, the arms are opened in second position. On 4, the position is held. On &, demi plié in second position; the left arm is closed in first position, the right one remains in second, the head and the focus remain en face. On 1 & of the second bar, the left leg, pushing away from the floor and maintaining the turnout of the heel, executes relevé on three-quarter point; the right leg, increasing the turnout of the upper part and of the heel, is raised to the conditional cou-de-pied position; the arms are united in first position. On 2 &, the

169

position on three-quarter point is held. On 3 &, the exercise is concluded in fifth position, épaulement croisé, in demi plié, right leg in front; the arms are opened, preserving their curve, the hands are opened forward, the head turns to the right. On 4 &, initial position.

Preparatory exercise for tour en dehors from fourth position
The preparatory exercise for tour en dehors from fourth position is at first studied en face. This exercise consolidates the correct position of the torso (with the hips level) and of the legs at the moment of the relevé. After mastering the preparatory exercise from fourth position, it is executed from épaulement croisé.

Initial position: fifth position épaulement croisé, right leg in front.

On the upbeat, demi plié in fifth position; the arms, opening slightly, return to the preparatory position. On 1 &, with a turn towards point 2 of the class diagram, a relevé on three-quarter point on the left leg, the right one is raised to the conditional cou-de-pied position; the arms are raised in first position, the head turns en face, the eyes are directed to the front (towards point 2). On 2 &, the position is held. On 3 &, the supporting leg executes demi plié; the working leg, increasing the turnout of the upper part, is drawn to the back and, straightening the knee, the foot is placed on the floor in fourth position; the left arm is opened in second position, the hands, opening, are turned with the palm facing downwards, assuming the third arabesque position. On 4, the position is held. On &, demi plié in fourth position. On 1 & of the following bar, the left leg, pushing away from the floor and increasing the turnout of the heel, executes relevé on three-quarter point; the right one, increasing the turnout of the upper part and of the heel, is raised to the conditional cou-de-pied position, the arms are united in first position. On 2 &, the position is held. On 3 &, the exercise is concluded in fourth position, épaulement croisé; the supporting leg executes demi plié, the working one is drawn backwards and, straightening the knee, is placed on the floor in fourth position; the arms are opened, preserving their curve, the hands are opened forward and the head turns to the left. On 4, the position is held.

Preparatory exercise for tour en dedans from fourth position
Initial position: fifth position épaulement croisé.

On the upbeat, demi plié in fifth position; the arms, opening slightly, return to the preparatory position. On 1 &, with a turn en face, relevé on three-quarter point with the left leg, the right one is raised to the conditional cou-de-pied position; the arms are raised in first position, the head turns en face, the eyes are directed to the front. On 2 &, the position is held. On 3 &, with a turn to épaulement croisé, the supporting leg executes demi plié; the working leg, increasing the turnout, is drawn to the back and, straightening the knee, it is placed on the floor in fourth position; the right arm is opened in second position, the left one remains in first, the head turns to the left. On 4 &, the position is held. On 1 & of the following bar, with a turn en face the left leg, increasing the turnout of the heel, executes relevé on three-quarter point; the right leg, increasing the turnout of the upper part and of the heel, is raised to the conditional cou-de-pied position; the arms are united in first position, the head turns en face, the eyes are directed to the front. On 2 &, the position is held. On 3 &, the exercise is concluded in fifth position, épaulement croisé, in demi plié, right leg in front; the arms are opened, preserving their curve, the hands are opened forward, the head turns to the right. On 4 &, initial position.

Preparatory exercise for tour en dehors from fifth position
Initial position: fifth position épaulement croisé, right leg in front.

The anacrusis is divided into three 1/8. On the first 1/8, the arms are opened; on the second, they are raised through the preparatory position into first, the head inclines towards the left shoulder, the eyes are directed towards the hands; on the third 1/8, demi plié in fifth position, with a turn en face, the left arm is opened in second position, the right one remains in first, the head turns en face and the eyes are directed to the front. On 1 &, the left leg, pushing away from the floor, executes a relevé on three-quarter point; the right one is raised to the conditional cou-de-pied position, the arms are raised in first position. On 2 &, the position is held. On 3 &, the right leg, increasing the turnout, comes down behind in fifth position demi plié, épaulement croisé; the arms are opened, preserving their curve, the hands are opened forward, the head turns to the left. On 4 &, initial position.

Preparatory exercise for tour en dedans from fifth position
Initial position: fifth position épaulement croisé, left leg in front.

The anacrusis is divided into three 1/8; on the first one, the arms are opened; on the second one, they are raised through the preparatory position into first; the head inclines towards the left shoulder, the eyes are directed towards the hands; on the third 1/8, demi plié in fifth position with a turn en face; the right arm is opened in second position, the left one remains in first, the head turns en face, the eyes are directed towards the front. On 1 &, the left leg, pushing away from the floor with the heel, executes a relevé on three-quarter point; the right one, increasing the turnout of the upper part and of the heel, is raised to the conditional cou-de-pied position; the arms are united in first position. On 2 &, the position is held. On 3 &, the right leg is put down in front in fifth position, demi plié, épaulement croisé; the arms are opened, preserving their curve, the hands are opened forward, the head turns to the right. On 4 &, initial position.

Remarks In the preparatory exercises for tours, the torso is 'pulled up', the shoulders are opened and lowered; during the relevé the legs are strongly held. The supporting leg must be turned out, with a stretched knee, and forcefully 'pulled up' at the hip; the working leg must be turned out and active as it is taken to the cou-de-pied. The preparatory exercise for tours, as well as the tours themselves, are executed in the middle and at the end of battement tendu, battement tendu jeté, battement fondu, battement frappé, etc.

The time signature is 4/4 at first, with the exercise executed in two bars. The character of the music is precise. Later on, the time signature depends on the exercise with which the preparatory exercise for tours is combined, but the character of the accompaniment for tours is maintained.

Tour en dehors from second position
Initial position: fifth position en face, right leg in front.

On the upbeat, demi plié in fifth position. On 1 &, relevé on three-quarter point in fifth position; the arms, opening slightly, are raised through the preparatory position into first, the head remains en face, the eyes are directed towards the front. On 2 &, the position is held. On 3 &, the right leg is opened to the side at 45°, the arms are opened in second position. On 4, the position is held. On &, the legs, without relaxing the muscles, come down into second position in demi plié; the right arm is closed in first position, the left one remains in second, the head remains en face, the eyes are directed towards the front. On 1 & of the second bar, tour en dehors; a turn of 360° on the left leg, to the right. During the tour the left leg, pushing away from the floor with the heel, executes a relevé on three-quarter point, with the knee forcefully stretched; the right leg is raised actively to the conditional cou-de-pied position, the left arm is united with the right one; the head turns to the left (the focus remaining fixed in the direction of point 1 of the class diagram) and as soon as possible, as if catching up with the turn, returns en face at the end of the tour. On 2 &, the turn is concluded but the position on three-quarter point is held. On 3 &, demi plié in fifth position, épaulement croisé, left leg in front; the arms are opened, preserving their curve, the hands are opened, the head turns to the left. On 4 &, initial position.

Tour en dedans from second position
Initial position: fifth position en face, left leg in front.

On the upbeat, demi plié in fifth position. On 1 &, relevé on three-quarter point in fifth position; the arms, opening slightly, are raised through the preparatory position into first; the head turns en face, the eyes are directed towards the front. On 2 &, the position is held. On 3 &, the right leg is opened to the side at 45°, the arms are opened in second position. On 4, the position is held. On &, the legs, without relaxing the muscles, come down in second position in demi plié, the left arm is closed in first position, the right one remains in second; the head remains en face, the eyes are directed towards the front. On 1 & of the second bar, tour en dedans, a turn of 360° on the left leg to the left. During the tour the left leg, pushing away from the floor with the heel, executes a relevé on three-quarter point, sending the heel forward; the knee is forcefully stretched, the right leg is raised actively to the conditional cou-de-pied position; the right arm is united with the left one in first position; the head turns to the right (the focus remaining fixed in the direction of point 1 of the class diagram), and as soon as possible, as if catching up with the turn of the torso, it returns en face at the conclusion of the tour. On 2 &, the tour is concluded but the position on three-quarter point is held. On 3 &, demi plié in fifth position, épaulement croisé, right leg in front; the arms are opened, preserving their curve, the hands are opened forward, the head turns to the right. On 4 &, initial position.

Remarks In tours the torso is 'pulled up', the weight of the body is centred exactly over the supporting leg, which is taut and turned out; when executing tour en dedans, the heel is particularly turned out. The working leg remains forcefully and actively sur le cou-de-pied. The arms maintain first position. The turn of the torso coincides exactly with that of the legs. A precise turn of the head and use of the focus stimulates the turn. The same device for turning is used when executing tours on point.

Pas de bourrée dessus-dessous
Initial position: fifth position, épaulement croisé, right leg in front.

Préparation on two introductory chords. On the first, the arms, opening slightly on the upbeat, are brought to the raised preparatory position; the head inclines towards the left shoulder, the eyes are directed towards the hands. On the second chord, with a turn en face, the right leg executes demi plié, the left one is stretched to the side at 45°, passing with a fleeting movement through the cou-de-pied derrière; the arms, preserving their curve, are opened into second position at half height, the hands are turned with the palms facing down, the head turns to the left (profile) and the eyes are directed towards the left hand. On 1, the left leg, sliding with the toe along the floor, steps onto three-quarter point, replacing the right leg in front, which is raised immediately sur le cou-de-pied derrière. The arms are raised through the preparatory position into first, the head turns en face. On 2, the right leg steps onto three-quarter point, travelling slightly sideways; the left leg is raised immediately sur le cou-de-pied derrière, the positions of the arms and head are held. On 3, the left leg executes demi plié, replacing the right one which is extended to the side at 45°, passing with a fleeting movement through the conditional cou-de-pied. The arms, preserving their curve, are opened in second position, the head turns to the right, the eyes are directed towards the right hand. On 4, the position is held, establishing the conclusion of the first part of the movement, that is pas de bourrée dessus (over).

On 1 of the second bar, the right leg, sliding with the toe along the floor, steps onto three-quarter point, replacing the left one at the back; this is raised immediately to the conditional cou-de-pied position, the arms are raised through the preparatory position into first, the head turns en face. On 2, the left leg steps over onto three-quarter point, travelling slightly sideways; the right leg is raised immediately to the conditional cou-de-pied position, the positions of arms and head are held. On 3, the right leg executes demi plié, replacing the left one which is opened to the side at 45°, passing with a fleeting movement through cou-de-pied derrière. The arms, preserving their curve, are opened in second position at half height; the hands are turned with the palms facing down, the head turns to the left, the eyes are directed towards the left hand. On 4, the position is held, establishing the conclusion of the second part of the movement, that is pas de bourrée dessous (under).

In pas de bourrée dessous-dessus the leg which is in front in fifth position is opened.

Remarks In pas de bourrée dessus-dessous the legs are taut and turned out, the torso is 'pulled up', the shoulders are opened and level, especially when executing demi plié.

Allegro

In allegro, jumps with a bouncing character are now introduced, with a short but very resilient demi plié. They develop the strength of the entire leg. They are executed on 1/8 notes. The study of bouncing jumps is begun in first position, then in second and, later on, on one leg with the other one sur le cou-de-pied devant or derrière. The alternating of resilient, soft jumps with bouncing ones develops the legs for high, light jumps.

175

Pas échappé in fourth position croisé

Initial position: fifth position, épaulement croisé, right leg in front.

The anacrusis is divided into three 1/8. On the first 1/8, the arms are opened slightly; on the second 1/8, demi plié in fifth position, the arms are closed into preparatory position; on the third 1/8, the legs push forcefully away from the floor, establishing fifth position in the air in a high jump; the arms are raised in first position and the head turns towards point 8 of the class diagram. On 1, the fully stretched legs, resisting the pull of gravity, open and come down in fourth position demi plié; the arms are opened in the small pose croisée, the head turns to the right. On &, the legs, without relaxing the muscles, push forcefully away from the floor, establishing fourth position in the air in a high jump, the arms and head remaining in the pose croisée. On 2 &, the fully stretched legs, resisting the pull of gravity, are joined together in the air in fifth position, demi plié; both arms are lowered into the preparatory position, the head remains turned to the right. On 3 &, the knees are straightened. 4 is the upbeat for the following échappé.

Pas échappé in fourth position effacé

Initial position: fifth position, épaulement croisé, right leg in front.

The anacrusis is divided into three 1/8. On the first 1/8, the arms are opened slightly; on the second 1/8, demi plié in fifth position, the arms are closed in the preparatory position; on the third 1/8, with a turn to effacé, the legs push forcefully away from the floor, establishing fifth position in the air in a high jump; the arms are raised in first position, the head turns towards point 2 of the class diagram. On 1, the fully stretched legs, resisting the pull of gravity, open and come down in fourth position demi plié; the arms are opened in the small pose effacée, the head turns to the left. On &, the legs, without relaxing the muscles, push forcefully away from the floor, establishing fourth position in the air in a high jump. The arms and head remain in pose effacée. On 2 &, the fully stretched legs, resisting the pull of gravity, are joined together in fifth position in the air and come down gradually into fifth position demi plié; the arms are lowered into the preparatory position, the head remains turned to the left. On 3 &, the legs are straightened. 4 is the upbeat for the following échappé. At the conclusion of the last échappé the legs, coming together in the air, are changed, coming down in épaulement croisé, left leg in front.

There are grands and petits échappés in fourth position croisé and effacé. Petit échappé is executed with a short, low jump, following all the given rules.

Remarks In demi plié in fifth and in fourth positions, the heels press firmly into the floor, with the legs fully turned out and the torso 'pulled up'. In the jump the legs are fully stretched; it is particularly important to remember this when executing a short, low jump. The torso is always 'pulled up' and calm, the arms, sustaining the pose, are free and easy.

The character of the musical accompaniment and the time signature are the same as for pas échappé in second position.

Temps levé

Temps levé is a short, strong jump, with a bouncing charcter it develops the strength of the entire leg and especially of the foot. At first, temps levé is combined with the simplest jump on one leg, which is sissonne simple.

Initial position: fifth position, épaulement croisé, right leg in front.

The anacrusis is divided into two 1/8. On the first 1/8, demi plié; on the second 1/8, the legs push forcefully away from the floor, establishing fifth position in the air in a high jump. On 1, the fully stretched legs resist the pull of gravity, the left leg executing demi plié, the right one assuming the conditional cou-de-pied position. On &, the left leg, repeating the jump, pushes forcefully away from the floor, stretching the knee, instep and toes; the right one, sustaining the turnout, remains sur le cou-de-pied. On 2, temps levé is concluded (resisting the pull of gravity) in demi plié on the left leg, the right one remaining sur le cou-de-pied. On & 3, the exercise is concluded with pas assemblé to the side, which is executed with the right leg passing from the cou-de-pied, with a fleeting movement through fifth position. On &, the legs are straightened in fifth position, left leg in front. 4 is the upbeat for the execution of the exercise with the other leg. Temps levé with the leg sur le cou-de-pied derrière is executed according to the same rules. Later on, the number of temps levés on one leg is increased to 2–3 times as many. Temps levé can be combined with pas jeté, pas échappé finishing on one leg, and with other movements.

Remarks During the jump the supporting leg is taut, the working leg is kept still, in a correctly placed and turned out cou-de-pied position. The arms, remaining in the preparatory position, are also calmly held.

The time signature is 4/4 or 2/4, the temps levés each taking 1/4.

Sissonne ouverte in poses

Sissonne ouverte in poses is studied after this movement has been mastered en face in all directions. On two introductory chords, the arms assume the small pose and on two concluding chords they are lowered into the preparatory position. Later on, sissonne ouverte in poses is executed with arm movements.

Example Sissonne ouverte in pose croisée devant.

Initial position: fifth position, épaulement croisé, right leg in front.

The anacrusis is divided into three 1/8. On the first 1/8, the arms are opened slightly. On the second 1/8, demi plié in fifth position, the arms return to preparatory position. On the third 1/8, the legs push away from the floor, establishing fifth position in a high jump, the arms are raised in first position and the head inclines slightly to the left. On 1, the left leg comes down in demi plié, the right one is opened at 45°, through the conditional cou-de-pied position, towards point 8 of the class diagram; the right arm is opened in second position, the left one remains in first, the head turns to the right (pose croisée). On &, the left leg pushes forcefully away from the floor in a vertical jump, the right leg is drawn towards the left one in fifth position in the air. On 2 &, the legs smoothly conclude sissonne ouverte in fifth position demi plié, the arms are lowered in preparatory position, the head remains turned to the right. On 3 &, the legs are straightened. 4 is the upbeat for the repeat of the jump.

Remarks Sissonne ouverte in the pose croisée derrière and in the poses effacée devant and derrière is executed according to the same rules, observing the particular characteristics of each pose. Sissonnne ouverte in écartée is executed with the arms opened in second position, similarly to sissonne ouverte to the side. The leg which is opened during the jump is directed exactly croisée, effacée or écartée, especially in the poses derrière. The torso is 'pulled up', the legs are fully turned out. The arms in the poses are held without strain.

The time signature is 4/4. The character of the musical accompaniment is energetic and precise. At first, the movement is executed in one bar, with pauses; later on without pauses, on a 2/4 time.

Sissonne fermée in poses

Sissonne fermée in poses is studied after this movement has been mastered en face in all directions. On two introductory chords, the arms assume the small pose and on two concluding chords, they are lowered into the preparatory position. Later on, sissonne fermée in poses is executed with arm movements.

Example Sissonne fermée en avant in pose croisée.

Initial position: fifth position, épaulement croisé, right leg in front.

The anacrusis is divided into three 1/8. On the first 1/8, the arms are opened slightly. On the second 1/8, demi plié in fifth position, the arms are raised through the preparatory position into first, the head inclines slightly to the left. On the third 1/8, the legs, pushing forcefully away from the floor, are opened in a high jump (the right leg to the front, the left one to the back), travelling in the air as far as possible towards point 8 of the class diagram; the right arm is opened in second position, the left one remains in first, the head turns to the right (pose croisée derrière). On 1 &, the legs, without relaxing the muscles, conclude sissonne fermée on the spot indicated by the pointed toes of the right leg, closing simultaneously in fifth position demi plié. On 2 &, the legs are straightened slowly, the arms remaining in the assumed position. On 3 &, the position is held. 4 & serves as upbeat for the following sissonne fermée en

179

avant. With the concluding demi plié, the arms are lowered in preparatory position, the head remains turned to the right.

At the beginning of the jump, the leg which opens to the front plays an active part. At the conclusion of the jump, the leg which is opened to the back plays an active part: sliding with the toe along the floor, it finishes sissonne fermée by joining the other leg in fifth position. The lightly held and 'pulled up' torso follows in the direction of the leg which is thrown to the front. The legs are turned out to the utmost.

Remarks Sissonnes fermées en arrière in the pose croisée and in the poses effacée en avant and en arrière are executed according to the same rules, observing the special characteristics of each pose. Sissonne fermée in écartée is executed with the arms in the small poses écartées.

The time signature is 4/4, later on 2/4. The character of the music is precise and energetic. At first, sissonne fermée is executed with pauses; later on without pauses, taking 1/4 for each sissone.

Pas jeté porté

Pas jeté porté sideways Initial position: fifth position épaulement croisé, right leg in front.

On 1, demi plié in fifth position; the arms, opening on the upbeat, are brought to the raised preparatory position; the head inclines to the left, the eye direction coincides with the inclination of the head. On &, with a turn en face, the right leg is opened to the side with a brushing movement, simultaneously with a high jump of the left leg, and travelling as far as possible in the direction of the toe of the right leg. The arms are opened in second position, the head turns en face. On 2, the jeté is concluded on the right leg, in demi plié, épaulement croisé; the left leg assumes the conditional cou-de-pied position, the arms are closed in preparatory position, the head inclines slightly to the right, the eye direction coinciding with the inclination of the head. On &, the position is held. On 3 &, the right leg is straightened, the left one is placed in fifth position behind, the head turns to the left. On 4 &, the position is held.

Pas jeté porté sideways is also executed from fifth position, starting with the back leg.

Initial position: as described above.

On 1, demi plié in fifth position; the arms, opening on the upbeat, are brought to the raised preparatory position, the head inclines to the left, the eye direction coinciding with the inclination of the head. On &, with a turn en face, the left leg is opened to the side with a brushing movement, simultaneously with a high jump of the right one, and travelling as far as possible in the direction of the toe of the left leg. The arms are opened in second position, the head turns en face. On 2, pas jeté is concluded on the left leg, in demi plié, épaulement croisé; the right one assumes the cou-de-pied derrière position; the arms are closed in preparatory position, the head turns to the right, the eye direction coincides with the turn of the head. On &, the position is held. On 3 &, the left leg is straightened, the right one is placed in fifth position behind, the head turns to the left. On 4 &, the position is held (fig. 60).

Pas jeté porté travelling forward Initial position: fifth position épaulement croisé, right leg in front.

On 1, demi plié in fifth position, the arms are opened on the upbeat and brought to the raised preparatory position; the head inclines to the left, the eye direction coinciding with the inclination of the head. On &, the right leg is opened forward, in croisé, with a brushing movement, simultaneously with a high jump of the left one, and travelling as far as possible in the direction of the toe of the right leg; the arms are opened in the direction of

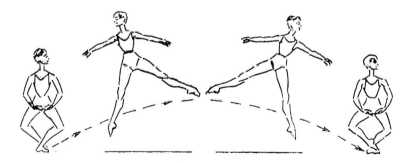

fig. 60   Pas jeté porté to the side (de côté)

181

second position, preserving their curve, the hands are opened forward, the head turns to the right. On 2, pas jeté is concluded on the right leg in demi plié, the left one assumes the cou-de-pied derrière position, the arms and head remain in the assumed positions. On &, the position is held. On 3 &, the right leg is straightened, the left one is placed in fifth position behind, the arms are closed in preparatory position, the head remains turned to the right. On 4 &, the position is held.

Pas jeté porté travelling backwards Initial position: as described above.

On 1, demi plié; the arms, opening on the upbeat, are brought to the raised preparatory position, the head inclines to the left, the eye direction coinciding with the inclination of the head. On &, the left leg is opened backwards, in croisé, with a brushing movement, simultaneously with a high jump of the right one, and travelling as far as possible in the direction of the toe of the left leg; the arms are opened in the direction of second position, preserving their curve, the hands are opened forward, the head turns to the right. On 2, pas jeté is concluded on the left leg in demi plié, the right one assumes the conditional cou-de-pied position, the arms and head remain in the assumed positions. On &, the position is held. On 3 &, the left leg is straightened, the right one is placed in fifth position in front, the arms are closed in preparatory position, the head remains turned to the right. On 4, the position is held.

Remarks In pas jeté porté in all directions, the 'pull up' of the torso helps the impetus of the movement. The legs are taut and turned out during the jump.

Later on, pas jeté porté is concluded by means of pas assemblé, which is executed on the count of & 3, with the leg passing from the cou-de-pied through fifth position in front or behind, depending on the conclusion of the pas jeté itself.

Later still, various directions of jeté porté are used in one and the same exercise. For example: jeté porté travelling sideways is executed with the front leg, starting from fifth position; after that, one does jeté porté croisé forward from the conditional cou-de-pied and the movement is concluded with pas assemblé derrière, executing it with the right leg, passing from the coup-de-pied through fifth position behind.

Sissonne tombée

Sissonne tombée en avant Sissonne tombée is a falling jump. Initial position: fifth position, épaulement croisé, right leg in front.

On 1, demi plié in fifth position; the arms, opening on the upbeat, return to the preparatory position, the head inclines slightly to the left. On &, the legs, pushing away from the floor, establish fifth position in a high jump, with pointed toes; the arms are raised in first position, the head turns en face, the eyes are directed to the front. On 2, the left leg comes down in demi plié, resisting the pull of gravity, and immediately the right leg is opened to croisée devant, passing with a fleeting movement through the conditional cou-de-pied position and, sliding with the toe along the floor, it transfers to demi plié; the left one is stretched behind in croisée, with the toe on the floor. The 'pulled up' body inclines forward, imparting a falling character to the jump. The right arm is opened in second position, the left one remains in first, the hands are opened, the head remains in the assumed position, the eyes are directed towards the left hand. On &, a jump on the right leg; the left one is drawn towards it in fifth position in the air while travelling forward. On 3 &, sissonne tombée is concluded in fifth position demi plié, the arms are in the preparatory position. On 4, initial position (fig. 61).

fig. 61   Sissonne tombée en avant

Sissonne tombée en arrière Initial position: as described above.

On 1, demi plié in fifth position, the arms, opening slightly on the upbeat, return to the preparatory position, the head inclines slightly to the left. On &, the legs, pushing away from the floor, establish fifth position in a high jump, with stretched toes; the arms are raised in first position, the head is brought upright, turning en face, with the eyes directed to the front. On 2, the right leg comes down in demi plié, resisting the pull of gravity, the left leg is opened to croisée derrière with a fleeting movement through the cou-de-pied derrière and, sliding with the toe along the floor, transfers to demi plié; the right one is stretched croisé devant with the toe on the floor. The 'pulled up' torso, slightly bending back at the waist starting with the upper back, imparts a falling quality to the jump. The right arm is opened in second position, the left one remains in first, both hands are opened, the head inclines slightly to the left, the eyes are directed towards the left hand. On &, a jump on the left leg; the right one is drawn towards it in fifth position in the air while travelling backwards. On 3 &, sissonne tombée is concluded in fifth position, demi plié, the arms are closed into the preparatory position. On 4 &, initial position.

Sissonne tombée de côte Initial position: as described above.

On 1, demi plié in fifth position; the arms, opening slightly on the upbeat, return to the preparatory position, the head inclines slightly to the left. On &, the legs, pushing away from the floor, establish fifth position in a high jump, with stretched toes; the arms are raised in first position, the head turns en face, the eyes are directed to the front. On 2, the left leg comes down in demi plié en face, resisting the pull of gravity; the right leg is opened in second position, passing with a fleeting movement through the conditional cou-de-pied and, sliding with the toe along the floor, transfers to demi plié; the left leg is stretched in second position with the toe on the floor. The 'pulled up' torso inclines to the right, imparting a falling character to the jump. The arms are opened in the direction of second position, the head turns to the right. On &, a jump on the left leg, the right one is drawn towards it in fifth position in the air while travelling to the side. On 3 &, sissonne tombée is concluded in fifth position, demi plié, the arms are closed into the preparatory position. On 4 &, initial position.

Sissonne tombée de côté is also executed with the leg standing in fifth position behind. In this case the leg is opened to the side, through the cou-de-pied derrière. If the jump is executed with the right leg, the head turns to the right at the moment of the tombé.

Remarks In sissonne tombée the legs are completely turned out and fully stretched, establishing fifth position in the air. The demi plié is resilient; the torso, 'pulled up' and light, is placed exactly over the supporting leg.

The time signature is 4/4: later on 3/4.

Pas ballonné
Pas ballonné de côté Initial position: fifth position en face, right leg in front.

On 1, demi plié in fifth position; the arms, opening on the upbeat, are raised through the preparatory position into first, the head inclines slightly to the left, the eyes are directed towards the hands. On &, the left leg is extended with a brushing movement, in second position, at 45°, simultaneously with a high jump of the left leg, travelling in the air towards point 3 of the class diagram. The arms are opened in second position, the head turns en face, both legs are taut. On 2, resisting the pull of gravity, ballonné is concluded in demi plié, on the left leg; the right leg is bent in the conditional cou-de-pied position, the right arm is closed in first position, the left one remains in second, the head turns to the right. On &, ballonné is repeated in the same direction while the right leg is opened during the jump to second position at 45°, directly from the cou-de-pied. The arms are opened in second position, the head turns en face, both legs are taut. On 3, resisting the pull of gravity, ballonné is concluded in demi plié on the left leg; the right leg is bent sur le cou-de-pied derrière, the left arm is closed in first position, the right one remains in second, the head turns to the left etc.

Ballonné is continued, alternating sur le cou-de-pied devant and derrière and changing the positions of arms and head. The movement is concluded with pas assemblé de côté or croisé derrière, lowering the arms in preparatory position (fig. 62).

fig. 62   Pas ballonné a côté

Pas ballonné effacé devant Initial position: fifth position, épaulement croisé, right leg in front, the arms are in the preparatory position, the head is turned to the right.

On 1, demi plié in fifth position; the arms, opening on the upbeat, are raised through the preparatory position into first, the head inclines to the left, the eyes are directed towards the hands. On &, with a turn to effacé, the right leg, increasing the turnout, is extended to effacé devant at 45° with a brushing movement, simultaneously with a high jump of the left leg and travelling in the air towards point 2 of the class diagram. In the jump, the right arm is opened in second position, the left one remains in first, the head turns to the left, both legs are taut (the small pose effacée in the air). On 2, resisting the pull of gravity, ballonné is concluded in demi plié on the left leg; the right leg, increasing the turnout, is bent on the conditional cou-de-pied. On &, ballonné is repeated, while the right leg is opened in the jump to effacé devant, at 45°, directly from the cou-de-pied etc.

Ballonné is repeated the required number of times, concluding it with pas assemblé effacé devant; together with the assemblé the arms are lowered into the preparatory position. This movement can also be concluded with assemblé écarté derrière into fifth position, épaulement croisé.

Pas ballonné effacé derrière Initial position: as described above.

On 1, demi plié in fifth position; the arms, opening on the upbeat, are raised through the preparatory position into first, the head inclines to the left, the eyes are directed towards the hands. On &, with a turn to effacé, the left leg, increasing the turnout, is extended in effacé derrière at 45° with a brushing movement, simultaneously with a high jump of the right leg, and travels in the air towards point 6 of the class diagram. In the jump the right arm is opened in second position, the left one remains in first, the head turns to the left, both legs are taut (the small pose effacée derrière in the air). On 2, resisting the pull of gravity, ballonné is concluded in demi plié on the right leg; the left leg, increasing the turnout, is bent sur le cou-de-pied derrière. On &, ballonné is repeated while the left leg is opened during the jump in effacé derrière, at 45°, directly from the cou-de-pied derrière etc. Ballonné is repeated the required number of times, concluding it with assemblé effacé derrière: together with the assemblé, the arms are lowered into the preparatory position. This movement can also be concluded with pas assemblé écarté devant into fifth position, épaulement croisé.

Pas ballonné croisé devant and derrière is executed according to the same rules, observing the character of the pose.

Remarks At first pas ballonné is studied to the side, facing the barre, and only after having mastered the stretching of the legs during the jump is it transferred to the centre. Here pas ballonné de côté, and in the poses croisée and effacée, are at first studied without travelling, two at a time. Gradually the number of ballonnés is increased. The demi plié after each jump must be resilient and short and the legs in the jump must be turned out. The positions of arms and head must be exact, the torso is 'pulled up', assisting the push away from the floor as well as the travelling. The arms remain in the pose, freely and easily held, without jerking during the jump.

The time signature is 4/4 or 2/4. Each ballonné is executed on 1/4. The character of the accompaniment is energetic and light.

Pas de chat

In the classical dance there are two kinds of pas de chat.

Pas de chat throwing the legs backwards Initial position: fifth position, épaulement croisé, right leg in front.

On 1, demi plié in fifth position; the arms, opening, are raised through the preparatory position into first, the head inclines to the left, the eyes are directed towards the hands, the 'pulled up' torso inclines slightly forward. On &, the left leg is thrown up behind at 45°, as in attitude croisé, and immediately the right leg, pushing away from the floor in a high jump, is also thrown up at 45° as in attitude croisé, while the torso bends back; the left arm is opened in second position, the right one remains in first, the hands, opening, are turned with the palms facing downwards, the head turns to the right: the pose is established in the air. On 2 &, pas de chat is concluded in demi plié, the right leg, delaying slightly, comes down in front in fifth position, the torso, arms and head remain in the assumed positions. On 3 &, the legs are straightened. On 4 &, initial position.

Remarks In its most perfect form, pas de chat demands an exact and precise co-ordination of the movements of the torso, arms and legs in the jump, with a soft and free design of the legs, imparting lightness to the jump. The inclination of the torso before the jump helps to bend back in the jump. The legs are thrown to the back but remain turned out. At first, pas de chat is studied without travelling, later on the jump is executed travelling forward.

Pas de chat, throwing the legs to the front Initial position: fifth position épaulement croisé, right leg in front.

On 1, demi plié in fifth position; the arms, opening slightly, are closed again into the preparatory position, the head is turned to the right. On &, the left leg is raised sur le cou-de-pied derrière; immediately the right leg, pushing away from the floor in a high jump while travelling forward, is raised to the conditional cou-de-pied; the arms are raised in first position, the head turns en face, the eyes are directed towards the hands and the pose is fixed in the air. On 2 &, pas de chat is concluded in demi plié while the right leg, delaying slightly, comes down in front in fifth position; the right arm is opened in second position and both hands are slightly opened forward with the eyes directed towards the left hand. On 3 &, the legs are straightened. On 4 &, initial position.

Remarks Here, just as in the first kind of pas de chat, an exact coordination of the movements of torso, arms and legs in the jump is demanded. The legs, bent in the air to establish the jump, must maintain their turnout. Pas de chat, throwing the legs to the front, is studied immediately travelling forward.

The time signature is 4/4. Pas de chat is executed in one bar. Later on, when the time signature is 2/4, the movement is still executed in one bar; when it has been mastered, it is executed taking 1/4 for each one.

Temps lié sauté
Temps lié consists of a series of sissonnes tombées in different directions. The jump retains the characteristics of temps lié, which demands a smooth and flowing execution. That is why in this jump it is not the falling, but the sliding character of the movement which is accentuated.

Temps lie sauté en avant Initial position: fifth position, épaulement croisé, right leg in front.

The anacrusis is divided into three 1/8. On the first 1/8, the arms are opened. On the second 1/8, demi plié in fifth position; the arms return to the preparatory position, the head inclines slightly to the left. On the third 1/8, the legs, forcefully pushing away from the floor, establish fifth position in a high jump; the arms are raised in first position, the head turns en face, the eyes are directed forward. On 1, the left leg, resisting the pull of gravity, comes down in demi plié; the right one opens in croisé devant with a fleeting movement through the conditional cou-de-pied and, sliding with the toe along the floor and lengthening the movement, it transfers to demi plié; the left leg is stretched in croisé derrière, touching the floor with pointed toes. The torso, retaining the 'pull up', is projected forward, the right arm is opened in second position, the left one remains in first, the hands are opened forward, the head remains in the assumed position, the eyes are directed towards the left hand. On &, a jump with the right leg, travelling slightly forward, the left leg is drawn immediately towards the right one in fifth position in the air. On 2, the legs conclude the jump with resilience in fifth position demi plié, épaulement croisé; the arms are lowered smoothly into the preparatory position, the head turns to the right. On &, simultaneously with a turn en face, the legs establish fifth position in a high jump, the arms are raised in first position, the head turns en face. On 3, the left leg, resisting the pull of gravity, comes down in demi plié; the right one is opened to the side, passing with a fleeting movement through the conditional cou-de-pied; sliding with the toe along the floor and lengthening the movement, it transfers to demi plié; the left leg is stretched in second position, touching the floor with pointed toes. The torso, retaining the 'pull up' and keeping the hips level, inclines to the right. On &, the right leg jumps up, travelling slightly to the right, the left leg is drawn towards the right one in fifth position in the air. On 4, the legs conclude the jump with resilience in fifth position demi plié, épaulement croisé, left leg in front. The arms are lowered smoothly into the preparatory position, the head turns to the left. '&' is the upbeat for temps lié sauté en avant with the left leg.

Temps lié sauté en arrière Initial position: fifth position épaulement croisé, right leg behind.

The anacrusis is divided into three 1/8. On the first 1/8, the arms are opened. On the second 1/8, demi plié in fifth position, the arms returning to the preparatory position. On the third 1/8, the legs, pushing forcefully away from the floor, establish fifth position in the air in a high jump; the arms are raised in first position, the head turns en face. On &, the left leg comes down in demi plié, the right one is opened in croisé derrière with a fleeting movement through the cou-de-pied derrière and, sliding with the toe along the floor, lengthening the movement, it transfers to demi plié; the left leg is stretched in croisé devant, touching the floor with pointed toes. The torso, retaining the 'pull up', bends back slightly, the left arm is opened in second position, the right one remains in first, the head inclines to the left. On &, a jump with the right leg, travelling slightly backwards; the left leg is drawn immediately towards the right one in fifth position in the air. On 2, the legs conclude the jump with resilience in fifth position demi plié, épaulement croisé; the arms are lowered smoothly in preparatory position, the head turns to the left. On &, simultaneously with a turn en face, the legs fix fifth position in a high jump, the arms are raised in first position, the head turns en face. On 3, the left leg comes down in demi plié, resisting the pull of gravity; the right one is opened to the side with a fleeting movement through the cou-de-pied derrière and, sliding with the toe along the floor, lengthening the movement, it transfers to demi plié; the left leg is stretched in second position, touching the floor with pointed toes. The torso, retaining the 'pull up' and keeping the hips level, inclines to the right; the arms are opened in second position, the head turns to the right. On &, a jump with the right leg, travelling slightly to the right, the left leg is drawn towards the right one in fifth position in the air. On 4, the legs conclude the jump with resilience in fifth position, demi plié, épaulement croisé, right leg in front. The arms are lowered smoothly into preparatory position, the head remains turned to the right. '&' is the upbeat for temps lié sauté en arrière with the left leg.

Remarks In temps lié sauté the legs are fully turned out in all positions and they are fully stretched in the jump. The demi plié is resilient and uninterrupted; the sliding movement of the toe along the floor is as wide as possible, the torso is 'pulled up' and light. The jump is co-ordinated precisely with the movements of arms, torso and head.

In the musical accompaniment, staccato and legato are alternated. The time signature is 4/4. Later on another possibility is 3/4.

Echappé battu from second position
Batterie is the beating of the legs against each other in the air.

Initial position: fifth position, épaulement croisé, right leg in front.

The anacrusis is divided into three 1/8. On the first 1/8, the arms are opened slightly; on the second 1/8, demi plié in fifth position, the arms are closed in the preparatory position; on the third 1/8, the legs push away from the floor, establishing fifth position in the air in a low jump; the arms are brought to the raised preparatory position, the torso and head turn en face. On 1, the legs come down in second position in demi plié, the arms are opened in the direction of second position, the head turns to the right. On &, the legs, pushing away from the floor from second position, remaining taut and turned out, beat against each other in the air (the right one in front, the left one behind) and, opening slightly after the beat, they are changed, increasing the turnout. On 2, demi plié in second position, left leg in front, the arms are closed in the preparatory position, the head turns to the left. On 3 &, initial position. 4 is the upbeat for échappé battu with the left leg.

Remarks In the beat, the legs beat against each other (especially the upper part) with equal strength and activity. After the beat the legs are opened exactly to the side.

The time signature is at first 4/4, later on 2/4, taking one échappé battu to a bar. The character of the music is energetic and precise.

Tour en l'air

The preparatory exercises for tour en l'air with a full turn begin with changement de pieds with a quarter turn.

> *Example* Initial position: fifth position en face, right leg in front, arms in the preparatory position.
>
> On 1, demi plié. On &, a high jump with a turn towards point 3 of the class diagram. The taut legs are changed according to the rules for changement de pieds. On 2 &, the turn is concluded in fifth position demi plié, left leg in front, with the head turned to the left. On 3 &, the legs are straightened. On 4 &, fifth position is held. On the following bar, a turn towards point 5 of the class diagram is executed etc.

Having mastered a quarter turn changement de pieds, half a turn (180°) is studied. The rules of the turn remain the same. The arms in the preparatory position are held without strain.

Remarks In the turn it is very important to observe the exact positions of shoulders and hips, and a precise turn of the head without tension in the neck. The arms are held freely and easily during the turn.

Turn of 360° Initial position: fifth position en face, right leg in front.

On the upbeat, the arms are raised in first position. On 1, demi plié in fifth position; the left arm is opened in second position, the right one remains in first, the eyes are directed to the front. On &, a high jump with a full turn in the air to the right; the left arm is united with the right one in first position, the head turns to the left (the eyes remain directed at point 1 of the class diagram) and as soon as possible, as if catching up with the turn of the torso, it returns en face at the conclusion of the turn.

The taut legs, preserving the turnout, are changed so that the left leg is in front in fifth position. On 2 &, tour en l'air is concluded in fifth position demi plié épaulement croisé, left leg in front; the arms are opened to the side, the hands are opened forward, the head turns to the left. On 3 &, initial position. 4 is the upbeat for the execution of the tour to the left.

Remarks Before the tour the heels push forcefully away from the floor. At the moment of the jump the legs, opening slightly according to the rules for changement de pieds, are closed forcefully in fifth position, stimulating the turn. In the tour the torso is 'pulled up', the legs are taut and turned out. The sharp turn of the head and the exact co-ordination of the arms stimulate the turn.

Exercices sur les pointes

Pas de bourrée dessus-dessous on point is executed according to the same rules as those for the execution on demi-point. The musical accompaniment is similar.

Pas jeté on point (not travelling)
Initial position: fifth position épaulement croisé, left leg in front.

On 1, demi plié in fifth position; the arms, opening on the upbeat, are returned to the preparatory position. On &, with a turn en face, the right leg is extended to the side with a sliding movement, the arms are opened in second position, the head turns to the right. On 2, the extended right leg, sliding with the toe along the floor, steps onto point in front of the left leg, as if replacing it. The left foot is raised immediately sur le cou-de-pied derrière, the right arm is closed in first position, the left one remains in second, the head is turned to the right. On &, the position is held. On 1 of the second bar, the left leg comes down and both legs execute demi plié in fifth position; the arms are lowered into the preparatory position, the head remains turned. On &, the left leg is extended to the side and pas jeté is executed with the other leg.

Pas jeté (not travelling) in the opposite direction Initial position: fifth position épaulement croisé, right leg in front.

On 1, demi plié in fifth position; the arms opening on the upbeat, are returned to the preparatory position. On &, with a turn en face, the right leg is extended to the side, the arms are opened in second position, the head turns to the left. On 2, the extended right leg, sliding with the toe along the floor, steps onto point behind the left leg, as if replacing it. The left leg is raised immediately to the conditional cou-de-pied, the right arm is closed in first position, the left one remains in second, the head is turned to the left. On &, the position is held. On 1 of the second bar, the left leg comes down and both legs execute demi plié in fifth position; the arms are lowered in preparatory position, the head remains turned. On &, the left leg is extended to the side and pas jeté is repeated with the other leg.

Remarks In pas jeté the torso is 'pulled up' and calm, especially when the leg is drawn under. The leg slides to and returns from second position exactly in a straight line. The legs are turned out in all positions and, when on point, the supporting leg is taut.

The character of the musical accompaniment is a combination of legato (demi plié) and staccato (jeté). The time signature is 2/4. Pas jeté is executed in one bar. Later on, pas jeté starts on the upbeat; on 2, demi plié in fifth position; on &, the leg slides to the side; on 1, it steps onto point; on &, the position is held.

Echappé in fourth position croisé

Initial position: fifth position, épaulement croisé, right leg in front.

On the upbeat, demi plié in fifth position. The arms, opening on the upbeat, are raised through the preparatory position into first; the head inclines to the left, the eyes are directed towards the hands. On &, the legs, opening simultaneously and uniformly, execute a relevé on point in fourth position. The right arm is opened in second position, the left one remains in first, the head turns to the right. On 2 &, the legs close simultaneously in fifth position demi plié, the arms and head remain in the assumed positions. On 3 &, the legs are straightened, concluding the movement. On 4 &, demi plié in fifth position. On 1 & of the following bar, échappé in fourth position etc until the end of the musical phrase. The arms are lowered in preparatory position with the last échappé.

Echappé in fourth position effacé

Initial position: fifth position, épaulement croisé, right leg in front.

On the upbeat, demi plié in fifth position. The arms, opening, are raised through the preparatory position into first, the head inclines slightly to the left, the eyes are directed towards the hands. On 1 &, pas échappé in fourth position on point, with a turn of the torso effacé, the right arm is opened in second position, the left one remains in first, the head turns to the left. On 2 &, both legs close simultaneously in fifth position demi plié, épaulement effacé, the arms and head remain in the assumed positions. On 3 &, the legs are straightened, concluding the movement. On 4 &, demi plié. On 1 & of the following bar, échappé and so on until the end of the musical phrase. The arms are closed in preparatory position with the last échappé.

Remarks Echappé croisé and effacé are executed with the arms in the small and in the big poses. In addition to the basic poses, other variants of the arms are allowed: in pas échappé with the right leg in front, the left arm may be opened in second position while the right is in first, with the small pose, or in third, with the big pose. In either case, the head remains turned to the right and the torso is sent slightly forward, changing the character of the pose. During the exercise the torso is 'pulled up' and the legs are turned out.

The character of the musical accompaniment is very accurate. At first the time signature is 4/4 and pas échappé is executed in two bars, as indicated above. Later on, the time signature is 2/4 and échappé is executed in one bar.

Having mastered échappé on point in fourth position croisé and effacé, it is recommended to combine échappé with relevé in fourth position. It is necessary to sustain the turnout of the legs in fourth position demi plié and relevé, and the even distribution of the body weight over both legs, and to ensure that the shoulders and hips are level.

Pas jeté on point (travelling)

Pas jeté croisé travelling forward Initial position: fifth position, épaulement croisé, right foot in front.

The anacrusis is divided into three 1/8. On the first 1/8, the arms are opened. On the second 1/8, the left leg executes demi plié, the right one is raised to the conditional cou-de-pied, the arms are brought to the raised preparatory position. On the third 1/8, the right leg is extended in croisé devant, at 45°; the left one remains in demi plié, the arms are raised in first position, the head inclines to the left, the eyes are directed towards the hands. On 1, the right leg, lengthening the movement, steps onto point; the left one is raised sur le cou-de-pied derrière, the right arm is opened in second position, the left one remains in first, the head turns to the right. On &, the position is held. On 2, the left leg comes down in demi plié, replacing the right one which is raised in the conditional cou-de-pied. The position of the arms is held, the head inclines to the left, the eyes are directed towards the left hand. On &, the right leg is opened croisée devant at 45°, the positions of the arms and head are held. On 1 of the following bar, the right leg, lengthening the movement, steps onto point, the head turns to the right and the exercise is continued. Pas jeté is concluded in fifth position demi plié, épaulement croisé, the arms are lowered into the preparatory position.

Pas jeté on point croisée en arrière is executed according to the same rules, from fifth position, starting with the back leg. The leg which opens in croisé derrière passes through the cou-de-pied derrière. In pas jeté croisé en avant, and particularly en arrière, it is necessary to maintain the 'pull up' of the torso.

Pas jeté in the poses effacée devant and derrière is executed according to the same rules.

Pas jeté croisé and effacé en avant and en arrière is executed with the arms in the small and in the big poses, but other variants of the arms are also allowed.

Pas jeté on point, travelling to the side From point 7 to point 3 of the class diagram, with the right leg, and from point 3 to point 7 of the class diagram, with the left one.

Initial position: fifth position, épaulement croisé, right leg in front.

The anacrusis is divided into three 1/8. On the first 1/8, the arms are opened. On the second 1/8, a turn en face, the left leg is in demi plié, the right one is raised to the conditional cou-de-pied; the arms are raised in first position, the head inclines to the left, the eyes are directed towards the hands. On the third 1/8, the right leg is opened to the side at 45°, the left one remains in demi plié, the arms, preserving their curve, are opened in second position. On 1, the right leg, lengthening the movement, steps onto point on the spot indicated by the pointed toe, the left leg is bent in the conditional cou-de-pied; the right arm is closed in first position, the left one remains in second, the head turns to the right. On &, the position is held. On 2, the left leg comes down in demi plié, replacing the right one which is raised immediately sur le cou-de-pied derrière; the head and arms remain in the assumed positions. On &, the right leg is opened to the side at 45°, the right arm is opened in second position, the head remains turned to the right. On 1 of the following bar, the right leg, lengthening the movement, steps onto point on the spot indicated by the pointed toe; the left one is bent sur le cou-de-pied derrière. The left arm is closed in first position, the head turns to the left and jeté on point travelling to the side is continued, finishing in fifth position demi plié, épaulement croisé, left leg in front; the arms are lowered into preparatory position.

Remarks Pas jeté on point is executed with a 'pulled up', light torso. In the movement the legs are fully turned out; on point, they are taut. The demi plié is resilient, the step is as wide as possible.

The time signature is 2/4.

Pas échappé finishing on one leg
Initial position: fifth position, épaulement croisé, right leg in front.

The anacrusis is divided into two 1/8. On the first 1/8, the arms are opened. On the second 1/8, demi plié in fifth position. On 1, with a turn en face, the legs execute relevé on point in second position, opening simultaneously and uniformly. The arms are opened in the direction of second position, the head inclines slightly to the left, the eyes are directed towards the right hand. On &, the legs, increasing the turnout, come down in second position demi plié; the positions of arms and head are held. On 2, with a turn to épaulement croisé, relevé on point with the left leg; the right one is bent sur le cou-de-pied derrière. The right arm is closed through the raised preparatory position into first, the left one remains in second, the head turns to the left. The shoulders are lowered and opened. On &, both legs execute demi plié in fifth position, the arms are lowered into the preparatory position. On 3, the legs are straightened. 4 is the upbeat for échappé with the left leg (fig. 63).

Pas échappé finishing on one leg, in the opposite direction
Initial position: as described above.

The upbeat is divided into two 1/8. On the first 1/8, the arms

fig. 63   Pas echappé finishing on one leg

are opened. On the second 1/8, they are brought to the raised preparatory position simultaneously with demi plié in fifth position. On 1, with a turn en face, the legs execute relevé on point in second position, opening simultaneously and uniformly; the arms are opened in the direction of second position, the head inclines slightly to the left, the eyes are directed towards the right hand. On &, the legs, increasing the turnout, come down in second position demi plié; the positions of arms and head are held. On 2, with a turn to épaulement croisé, relevé on point on the right leg; the left one is bent in the conditional cou-de-pied; the right arm is closed in first position, the left one remains in second, the head turns to the left, the shoulders are lowered and opened. On &, both legs execute demi plié in fifth position, the arms are lowered into the preparatory position. On 3 &, the legs are straightened. 4 is the upbeat for échappé with the left leg.

Remarks In pas échappé finishing on one leg, the torso is 'pulled up', the shoulders are opened and lowered, the movements of the arms and head are free, and the legs are turned out in all positions.

The time signature is 4/4. The character of the musical accompaniment is very accurate and energetic.

Pas jeté fondu

This exercise is executed on a diagonal, travelling forward and backward from point 4 towards point 8 of the class diagram with the right leg, and from point 6 towards point 2 with the left leg.

Initial position: fifth position, épaulement croisé, right leg in front (at point 4 of the class diagram).

The anacrusis is divided into three 1/8, just as in pas jeté on point. On 1 &, the right leg, lengthening the movement croisé en avant, steps onto point; the left one, bending, is directed with pointed toes towards the right leg and, passing according to the principles for passé (but at the level of the cou-de-pied) on 2 &, it is extending in effacé devant, at 45°. At the same time, the right leg comes down smoothly in demi plié. On 1 &, the left leg, lengthening the movement effacé devant, steps onto point; the right one, bending, is directed with pointed toes towards the left leg and, passing, according to the rules for passé (but at the level of the cou-de-pied) on 2 &, it is stretched croisé devant at 45°. At the same time the left leg comes down smoothly in demi plié etc. until the end of the musical phrase, alternately croisé and effacé. Pas jeté fondu on the diagonal, travelling to the back from point 8 towards point 2 of the class diagram, is executed according to the same rules, beginning with the back leg, from fifth position and alternating croisé and effacé in the same manner.

Remarks In pas jeté fondu the torso is 'pulled up' and the body weight is centred exactly over the supporting leg. This facilitates the process of travelling. In all positions the legs are turned out. The resilience of the demi plié imparts a softness and smoothness to the movement. The 'pulled up' torso is inclined forward slightly at the beginning of the movement, but is brought upright while travelling; the arms are also gradually opened into the given position. The positions of the arms in pas jeté fondu en avant and en arrière may be varied; the position of the head depends on the position of the arms.

The time signature is 2/4 or 3/4, each movement is executed in one bar.

Pas échappé en tournant in second position with a quarter turn
Initial position: fifth position, épaulement croisé, right leg in front.

The anacrusis is divided into two 1/8. On the first 1/8, the arms are opened. On the second 1/8, they are closed in the preparatory position, simultaneously with demi plié in fifth position. On 1, the legs execute relevé on point in second position, with a turn towards point 3 of the class diagram, the head turning to the left. On &, the position is held. On 2 &, the legs, increasing the turnout, are closed in fifth position demi plié, left leg in front. The arms remain in the preparatory position, the head remains turned to the left. On 1 of the following bar, échappé is repeated with a turn towards point 5 of the class diagram, the head turns to the right etc. Échappé is continued until it reaches point 7, and is concluded facing point 1 of the class diagram.

Échappé en tournant turning to the left is executed facing points 7, 5, 3 and 1 of the class diagram.

The turn of the head coincides with the relevé and is held in the demi plié.

Remarks The turn of the torso must coincide exactly with the échappé, the legs are opened simultaneously and uniformly during the turn.

The time signature is 2/4, the movement is executed in one bar. The character of the music is light and energetic.

Pas glissade en tournant

Pas glissade en tournant with a half turn is studied travelling sideways, from point 7 towards point 3 of the class diagram with the right leg, and from point 3 towards point 7 with the left one. At first, pas glissade is studied on three-quarter point.

Initial position: fifth position en face, right leg in front; the arms are in the preparatory position, the head is turned to the right.

The anacrusis is divided into three 1/8. On the first 1/8, the arms are opened. On the second 1/8, demi plié in fifth; the arms are raised through the preparatory position into first, the left one, continuing the movement is opened in second position and the head turns to the right. On the third 1/8, the right leg is extended in the direction of point 3 of the class diagram with a sliding movement; the left one remains in demi plié. The right arm is opened in second position, the palms of both hands are facing downwards, the head remains turned to the right. On 1, with a turn of 180° to the right, the right leg steps onto point on the spot indicated by the pointed toe and the left leg is drawn immediately towards the right one in fifth position behind; the left arm is closed in first position, the right arm remains in second, the head turns to the left. On &, the position is held. On 2, demi plié in fifth position; the arms and head remain in the assumed positions. On &, the left leg is opened in the direction of point 3 of the class diagram, the left arm is opened in second position, the head remains turned to the left. On 1, with a turn of 180° to the right, the left leg steps onto point on the spot indicated by the pointed toe and the right leg is drawn immediately towards the left one in fifth position in front; the right arm is closed in first position, the left one remains in second, the head turns to the right and the movement is repeated (fig 64).

Pas glissade en tournant in the opposite direction
Initial position: as described above.

The anacrusis is divided into three 1/8. On the first 1/8, the

fig. 64   Pas glissade en tournant

arms are opened. On the second 1/8, demi plié in fifth position; the arms are raised through the preparatory position into first; the right arm, continuing the movement, is opened in second position, the head turns to the left. On the third 1/8, the left leg is stretched, with a sliding movement in the direction of point 7 of the class diagram, the right leg remains in demi plié; the left arm is opened in second position, the palms of both hands are facing downwards and the head remains turned to the left. On 1, with a turn of 180° to the right, the left leg steps onto point on the spot indicated by the pointed toe and the right leg is drawn immediately towards the left one in fifth position in front; the right arm is closed in first position, the left one remains in second, the head turns to the right. On &, the position is held. On 2, demi plié in fifth position, the arms and the head remain in the assumed positions. On &, the right leg is opened in the direction of point 7 of the class diagram, the right arm is opened in second position, the head remains turned to the right. On 1, with a turn of 180° towards the right, the right leg steps onto point on the spot indicated by the pointed toe and the left leg is drawn immediately towards the right one in fifth position behind; the left arm is closed in first position, the right one remaining in second, the head turns to the left and the movement is continued.

Remarks The turn of the torso must coincide precisely with the turn of the taut and turned out legs. The movements of the arms and head must be well co-ordinated.

The time signature is 2/4. The character of the music is precise and energetic.

Tour on point from fifth position
(See tours on demi-point.)